TOO YOUNG TO DIE:
INNER CITY
ADOLESCENT HOMICIDES

A Psychological Investigation

Dr. Earl Bracy

TOO YOUNG TO DIE: INNER CITY ADOLESCENT HOMICIDES:
A Psychological Investigation

Copyright © 2025 **Melanie Thurston**
First Edition

ISBN (Paperback): 978-1-964494-29-6
ISBN (Hardback): 979-8-89672-080-5
ISBN (Ebook): 978-1-964494-34-0

All rights reserved. No part of this book may be used or reproduced by any means, graphic, electronic, or mechanical, including photocopying, recording, taping or by information storage and retrieval system without the written permission of the author except in the case of brief quotations embodied in critical articles and reviews.

Because of the dynamic nature of the Internet, any web addresses or links contained in this book may have changed since publication and may no longer be valid. The views expressed in the work are solely those of the author and do not necessarily reflect the views of the publisher, and the publisher hereby disclaims any responsibility for them.

Printed in the United States of America.

5830 E 2nd St, Ste 7000 #9983
Casper, WY 82609
USA

The opinions expressed herein are those of the author who assumes complete and sole responsibility for them, and they do not necessarily represent the views of the publisher or its agents.

I would like to dedicate this work to several people who meant a great deal to me as they traveled life's journey upon this earth. Each one of them shared their wisdom with me and taught me how to live my life. Their deaths reinforced the fact that life is precious and short. It saddened me deeply to lose them, but at the same time, it gave me a deeper insight into why we're on this earth.

I dedicate this work to my sister, Joyce Bracy-Lewis, who died from breast cancer during my third year of graduate school. I admired her for her strong faith in God. This she practiced until the very end of her physical life on this earth. I also followed her lead in being a responsible and caring person.

Secondly, I dedicate this work to my Uncle Wilmer Matherson who died from multiple complications after heart surgery at the very end of my therapy practicum and on the same day as my comprehensive examination. My uncle graduated from the school of hard knocks, and he had a tremendous amount of inner strength, which I admired. He taught me that knowledge is power. I give much credit to him for propelling me to excel in my educational pursuits.

I also dedicate this work to my Uncle Claude Matherson who died during my first year of graduate school after a lengthy illness. He too possessed a great deal of inner strength and calm that I'm sure I emulated. His heart and his home were always open to me when I was a child and as an adult.

Last, but surely not least, I dedicate this work to my friend, mentor, and former employer, Dr. Richard T. Shore, a very gifted heart surgeon who died of a massive heart attack on Christmas Eve, 1994. He took me under his wing and provided expert tutelage and sound advice. He was gracious enough and understanding enough to allow me to continue my educational pursuits while being employed by him. He marveled as I grew into the person that I've become. He was truly one in a million.

I would first like to thank God for guiding my path and for giving me the vision and the insight to undertake this most important project. I would be remiss if I did not give thanks to my parents, Mr. Gayle Bracy and Mrs. Maxine Bracy, for the morals and values that they instilled in me at a very early age. Due to their love and concern, there has always been a sense of balance in my life.

I have worked closely with several adolescents who have committed a homicide, and I am grateful for the knowledge that I have gained through working with this very challenging population.

The physical presence of each one of these people will be truly missed, but while on this earth, my life and the lives of others were greatly enriched because of them. Each traumatic life experience brings with it an opportunity for us to develop new insights and a deeper vision of truth.

CONTENTS

Introduction..xi

CHAPTER 1
Review of the Literature: Theoretical Perspectives Related to
Inner-City Adolescent Homicides 1

CHAPTER 2
An Exploration of Contributing Psychological Variables......................16

CHAPTER 3
Discussion and Recommendations 66

Research References..83

About the Author..103

INTRODUCTION

BECAUSE OF THE escalating African American male homicide rate, many social scientists are beginning to feel that the African American male is becoming an endangered species (Gibbs, 1984). Terr (1989) posits that many of these homicides occur because many poor inner-city African American adolescent males feel alienated from a society that does not recognize them and is not making a place for them in society. This alienation and rejection can easily cause the adolescent to direct his anger and rage on to others just like him. Bell (1987) stated that for every homicide that occurred in Chicago, Illinois, there were forty-four assaults serious enough to warrant police intervention.

Much research has been done on aggressivity in adolescent boys. Chandler (1982) provides empirical evidence linking specific causal attributions to anger arousal. He found that anger is when an individual holds another person responsible for the negative or harmful consequences of a social transaction. He further stated that when a threat or potential harm is perceived, attributing blame to others may serve as a defensive emotion-focused coping strategy that fuels anger arousal and increases the likelihood of aggressive responding, particularly among impulsive, under-socialized adolescents.

Boone (1990) hypothesizes that parental use of physical punishment and other power-assertive disciplinary methods tend to increase the likelihood of the development of aggressive behavior in boys. He also states that boys reared in households lacking adequate nurturance and praise for positive behaviors are prone to display negative behavioral patterns. These aggressive tendencies can often lead to homicides. What is most alarming is that the victims and perpetrators are becoming much younger. According to the Bureau of Statistics, in 1993, there were 3,647 teenage murderers. In 2005, the bureau predicted that annually, 5,000 such murders will occur.

Also, according to this projection, young men and women between the ages of fourteen to seventeen will commit these murders. This surge will be the greatest among African Americans (National Center for Injury and Prevention Control, 1990).

Today, the leading cause of death among young African American males is homicide (Poussaint, 1984). Bell (1987) reports that the homicide rates for African Americans are six to seven times greater than they are for Caucasians. Poussaint (1984) states that the murderer is psychologically impaired because of the hostile environment in which he lives. He suggests that the impairment comes in the form of low self-esteem, low self-concept, and self-hatred. These variables, he implies, intertwine to interfere with rational thinking on the part of the perpetrator. Further, Griffin (1991) posits that humiliation caused by racism and substandard living conditions cause a great deal of anger and rage, thus causing the adolescent to violently act out toward those who look like him. Projected self-hatred facilitates blind rage and gives the perpetrator of the violent attack a sense of legitimacy and justification (Poussaint, 1984).

CHAPTER 1

REVIEW OF THE LITERATURE: THEORETICAL PERSPECTIVES RELATED TO INNER-CITY ADOLESCENT HOMICIDES

DEUSCH (1993) REPORTED that African American children had significantly more negative self-images than did white children. He maintained that among the influences converging on the African American urban child is his sensing that the larger society views him as inferior and expects a decreased performance from him as evidenced by the general denial to him of realistic vertical mobility possibilities. With this in mind, it is highly probable that many African American adolescents, both male and female, tend to see a future that is hopeless and bleak.

In response to this feeling of inferiority, it is highly probable that many of these adolescents undertake a course of self-destruction and destruction of others who remind them of themselves. Under these conditions, it is understandable that the African American adolescent would tend to question his own competencies and, in so questioning, would be acting largely as others expect him to act. Merton (1980) called this a "self-fulfilling prophecy." The very expectation itself is a cause of its fulfillment.

Oftentimes, parents tell their children that they will not amount to anything. The child in turn expects this to happen, and because he expects it to happen, often it will. The parents, consciously or unconsciously, have planted a seed of negativism. The child fulfills the prophecy that the parents have predicted for him. Many adolescents who are incarcerated report that they were told by their mothers that they would end up in prison. Others have said that family members told them that they would be in prisons just like their fathers. The adolescent may also expect to be incarcerated because most of his friends and peers have been or are incarcerated. He sees this as a rite of passage that has to be fulfilled. Also, if he thinks that society views him as someone to be feared and someone whose life is meaningless, he will fulfill this message through his deeds and behavior.

According to George Mead (1962), the self is formed through the individual's interaction with other members of society—his peers, parents, teachers, and other agents of socialization. In the case of the African American adolescent, he/she learns to assume the role and attitudes of others with whom he/she comes in contact. In the process, the adolescent forms a perception of self. When the "self" and those who resemble the "self" are seen in a negative light, destruction to the self and others can occur. This negativism and self-hatred, if you will, contribute a great deal to black-on-black violence (Poussaint, 1984).

One should also realize that the vast majority of inner-city African Americans strongly oppose crime and violence and do not accept them as their "norm." Curtis (1975) stated that a variety of historical and contemporary forces combine to produce a violent counterculture among low-income urban African Americans. He also posits that this counterculture is supported and reinforced by exaggerated aggressive masculine strivings by African American men who have been emasculated by institutional racist practices.

Silverstein and Krate (1975) studied African American males in Harlem and state that boys within their peer groups elaborated such personal traits as skill in fighting, physical bravery and daring, and an ability to outwit and verbally insult others. This behavior often provoked a violent response in others. The salient point that is made is that among low-income African Americans, as among other groups of similar stature, violence is sanctioned as an acceptable method of resolving conflicts and arguments.

What has been neglected in this exploration has been the analysis of the African American experience itself in a society that victimizes individuals because of skin color. In order to arrive at concrete intervention strategies, it is crucial to focus on the antecedent mindset of poor African Americans. Oppression has occurred in previous generations of older African Americans, and many of these oppressive symptoms have been passed down to the younger generation. Oppression has produced psychological scarring in many African Americans that may oblige them to be ready victims as well as victimizers (Poussaint, 1984).

Linehan (1989) stated that one of the greatest joys in life is to love and to be loved by others. When this emotion is not fulfilled, people often tend to act out in anger and rage. Young (1993) further stated that early maladaptive schemas can develop in childhood and result in maladaptive behavior, which reinforces the schema. Turner (1984) theorized that maladaptive schemas are reinforced over time that can further add to pathology.

Kardiner and Ovesey (1951) state that self-hatred is at the core of much African American behavior that is destructive to the self and the group. The self-hatred is a valuable theoretical construct because it lends credence to the concept of low self-esteem and rage among African

Americans. This theory is also consistent with other theories that suggest a lower threshold for rage and violence among African Americans. In this view, socioeconomic, environmental, and family stressors combine with self-hatred to foster and trigger violent acts and homicide, which turns into a vicious circle.

A number of more recent studies suggest that negative self-concept based on skin color is no longer a problem among African American adolescents (Bass et al. 1982). Despite recent controversy, the self-hatred thesis is an important variable in black-on-black homicide and deserves continued exploration (Poussaint, 1984).

Bach-y-Rita, et al. (1971), gave psychological profiles to forty-three violent patients and found that, dynamically, they were dependent men with poor masculine identity and a sense of being useless, impotent, and unable to change their environment Although most of these men were white, their basic self-image resembled one that is often attributed to African American men as a result of being poor and black (Clark, 1965; Grier and Cobbs, 1968).

In the Bach-y-Rita study, it was found that violent episodes by these men were marked by a temporary breakdown of ego function and a disorganization of the thought process often induced by enormous rage. Curtis (1975), after determining that African American male violence is rarely planned or based on old animosities, posed two questions that have relevance to low self-esteem and self-hatred: "What is it about street-corner male contexts that encourages head-to-head standoffs? Once begun, why do so many confrontations seemingly escalate into resolutions of serious injury or death?" One must take into consideration that the two critical variables in such confrontations are low self-esteem and self-hatred, which predispose these individuals to explosive sensitivity to slights and threats to their self-respect.

Bromberg (1961) reported that a derogatory remark about race, skin color, and social and economic success in life may be an adequate stimulus to lead a fragile frustrated individual to violence. Rose (1981) reports that black encounters involving loss of self-respect or lowering of self-esteem are likely to produce an intense emotional reaction that leads to arguments which quickly escalate into physical assault and homicide.

Shneidman (1976) talked about the concept of inimicality as it relates to suicide. He defines inimicality as "those qualities within the individual that are unfriendly toward the self." Allen (1980) posits that these self-antagonistic parts of the person have early beginnings, and the adversity strengthens through negative reinforcements. When the African American adolescent holds a negative view of himself and the world, his/her feelings are often reinforced by a negative and hostile environment. It is highly probable that those experiencing self-hatred or low self-esteem or low self-concept have no problem projecting those feelings onto others, especially others who look like themselves. As seen in Shneidman's (1976) theory of suicide, as inimicality increases, so does the risk for homicide.

Allen (1980) talked about the concept of perturbation. What he is referring to is what he calls a negative emotion and frustration that result from socioeconomic ills, poverty, poor housing, and a disorganized family system. When individuals feel powerless and hopeless, this increases the intensity of perturbation (Allen, 1980). Allen also suggests that if homicides are to be prevented, the perpetrator first must change his/her attitude toward the victim's existence. Many African American adolescent murderers have admitted that they felt no remorse about committing a murder. This may occur because they've been conditioned to become numb to emotional pain by the ugly environment in which they live. Secondly, it's possible the perpetrator is incapable of any feelings toward his/her victim because the victim is a mirror image of himself/herself, and society has repeatedly told him that this person is useless, negative, "bad," a menace to society, and hopeless.

This same behavior pattern can be seen in African American adolescent females as well because of the modeling phenomenon. What is taking place today is that the female adolescent will often-times emulate the behavior of her male counterpart. This type of activity or behavior, if you will, is quite prevalent in female gangs.

Bandura (1969) posits that social learning is explained in terms of a continuous reciprocal interaction between cognitive, behavioral, and environmental interactions. When the environment is harsh, people will tend to take on defensive tactics that will ensure their survival. When the African American adolescent finds himself/herself in such an environment, one such survival tactic may be equipping themselves with some sort of weapon. All too often in today's climate, the weapon of choice is a gun.

The act of carrying a weapon appears to be prevalent throughout society; however, from a statistical standpoint, it is apparent that the homicide rate is highest among African American males (Centers for Disease Control and Prevention, 1992). Because of this epidemic, the African American homicide rate has become the number one health problem in the African American community.

Paster (1985) states that often in the poor African American adolescent, psychopathology can be underdiagnosed, undertreated, and misunderstood. Paster further states that depression in African American males can be seen in acting out behavior, which can often be violent in nature. The literature does not fully address whether the perpetrator of homicides was depressed during the time the murder was committed. If this issue is explored in depth, it's possible that a great deal of rich information can be extracted.

Durant, et al. (1995), studied a group of adolescents living in and around a public housing project. What he looked at was exposure to violence and victimization and depression. Durant found that depression was positively correlated with corporal punishment, family conflict, and exposure to violence. He also looked at the socioeconomic status of the adolescent's family. Through the use of regression analysis, Durant found that with a lower socioeconomic status (SES), the adolescent had a much higher depression level. The increase in depression could have been caused by multiple variables, but the fact that socioeconomic status alone plays such a vital part is crucial in examining the possible depressogenic component involved in causing an adolescent to commit a murder.

Paster (1985) talks about depression in the unacculturated acting out African American male. The type of machismo or acting out that she refers to can in many instances be forms of masked depression. When clinicians tend to think of depression, it's generally thought of in a clinical sense, whereby there are vegetative signs. What's being proposed is that one does not have to be lethargic or listless to be depressed.

Paster (1985) further states that many of these at-risk adolescents have very few contacts with adult males in paternal roles. Their social skills can be very poor because they have almost no social contact with middle-class persons, except authority figures in school and other agencies. Many of these adolescents feel segregated, isolated, frustrated, angry, and alienated. Because of this, they will reject the larger society.

At the same time, these adolescents feel that the larger society is rejecting of them. Poussaint (1985) posited that the poor African American adolescent can see himself as someone to be feared or avoided. Paster (1985) also feels that there is a devaluing of self-worth in this population. As stated by Poussaint (1985), the perpetrator devalues the life of his victim because he sees a mirror image of himself.

The literature does adequately address the father's absence and how this absence impacts the life of the adolescent. Paster (1985) went on to say that the adolescent is forced to accept the harsher realities of life. He feels that his missing father does not care about him and will never appear lo claim paternity. It is highly probable that if the adolescent feels that no one cares about him, he will, in turn, care about no one.

Winnicott (1967) also addresses the importance of consistent love and emotional support from the mother. Boone (1990) posited that nonaggressive boys reported that their mothers were prone to express love toward them through emotional and psychological support. On the other hand, aggressive boys tended to view their mother's love in terms of material goods that were provided.

Winnicott (1967) talked about the "good enough mother." The good enough mother meets the omnipotence of the infant. Because of this, a true self is formed. It makes sense that this theory can be extended across time until the individual starts to individuate in late adolescence. If the "good enough" theory holds true for the mother, then a similar theory should apply for the "good enough father." The literature has adequately addressed the role of the father in the life of the African American adolescent. When an adolescent's emotional needs have been fully met by one or both parents, the deadness, worthlessness, depression, drug abuse, recklessness, anger, rage, and violent behavior tend not to exist. When the adolescent is vulnerable, he/she may succumb to pathological disorders that can cause self-destruction and destruction to others (Easson, 1977).

The Moynihan Report of 1965 has often been cited and criticized by many African Americans. In his report, he stated, "The family is the cornerstone of our society. More than any other force, it shapes the attitudes, the hopes, the ambitions, and the values of the child. When the family collapses, it is the children that are usually damaged. When it happens on a massive scale, the community itself is crippled. So unless we work to strengthen the family to create conditions under which most parents will stay together, all the rest: schools and playgrounds, public assistance and private concern, will never be enough to cut completely the circle of despair and deprivation."

Erickson (1963) states in Childhood and Society that "There is in every child at every stage, a new miracle of vigorous unfolding, which constitutes a new hope and new responsibility for all."

Whitehead (1993) states that what children need most is stable families. The evidence supports the fact that when children grow up with two parents, they do tend to excel. These children are also not as likely to fall prey to the social pathologies that afflict kids from one-parent families. Many good kids come from single-parent households, so one should not totally dismiss this population as being at risk. When we look at the national trends, 50 percent of all marriages end in divorce. In the inner city, this figure can hover around 80 percent.

As early as 1909, DuBois attempted to show that the lower status of African Americans was not due to genetics but instead had a great deal to do with oppressive living conditions and the negative effect of slavery. These variables contributed a great deal to the disorganization of the African American family. Fra?ier (1939) wrote: "The widespread disorganization of family life among Negroes has affected practically every phase of their community life and adjustments to the larger white world" (p. 364).

There are many who may argue that slavery is a thing of the past and that one should be concerned with the here and now. However, what is happening in the here and now also has roots in the past. Myrdal (1944) viewed the African American family as a poor or ill-defined replica of the white family. He also identified the African American family as pathological, like many other forces in the life of African Americans. Myrdal went on to say that "The instability of the Negro family, the inadequacy of educational facilities for Negroes, the emotionalism in the Negro church, the insufficiency and unwholesomeness of Negro recreational activity, the plethora of Negro sociable organizations, the narrowness of interests of the average Negro, the provincialism of his political speculation, the high Negro crime rate, the cultivation of the arts to the neglect of other fields, superstitions, personality difficulties and other characteristic traits are mainly forms of social pathology."

In spite of all of the negative things written about African American families, African American families have, for hundreds of years, survived insurmountable odds. Oftentimes, researchers focus on the negatives in the African American family and fail to mention the strengths. The strengths are what have enabled the African American family to survive.

In the mid-1960s, there was a shift in values, morals, and attitudes throughout America. When this shift occurred, people started to think in terms of "me." There was a great deal of hedonism, which included drug usage of every kind. More importantly, this is when the breakdown of the family occurred. It is highly probable that those children born in the late sixties and seventies were affected the most negatively. Those born in the 1980s have also been impacted tremendously. Time will only tell how much of an impact family disorganization has had on this generation.

The African American family, and especially the inner-city African American family, was hardest hit by this shift because of the preexisting fragility of these families. As the concept of the "me" generation took hold, so did the devastating effects of drugs.

Even though alcohol and other drugs are used predominantly by white America, crack cocaine and alcohol have helped to destroy African American neighborhoods. Many inner-city neighborhoods have become combat zones because of the prevalence of drugs and alcohol.

Harper (1976) states that "alcoholism is the number one health problem and the number one social problem in Black America." Additionally, the crack cocaine epidemic is probably the worst thing that has happened to the African American community since the institution of slavery (Staples, 1990). Not only can crack be debilitating, but it can fool the user into believing that he or she is invincible, that he or she is in control, and that the drug does not control them (Staples, 1990). Crack cocaine is a drug that can cause an already violent individual to become even more violent. Those taking the drug can also become extremely depressed and, at other times, euphoric. In the case of many homicides, the perpetrator has often engaged in polysubstance abuse. Each individual reacts differently to drugs. When the individual ingests a combination of drugs, it would be extremely difficult to predict that individual's behavior. In many instances, violence is manifested. This volatile drug combination is another variable that may be overlooked when studying inner-city African American male homicides.

Ebata (1990) also addresses the stress component as it relates to adjustment and coping by the African American adolescent in high-crime areas. Blood pressure has been measured in inner-city children as young as six years old, and it was found that many of these children had elevated blood-pressure readings because of the constant sound of police sirens and gunfire. This can be seen as a physiological response to stress. Life stress can also have a deleterious impact on the psychological adjustment of adolescents and has been reported to be associated with depression, suicide, violence, and other delinquent behavior (Cohen, 1985). When an adolescent is exposed to violence in the home and in his/her neighborhood, this is thought to be extremely stressful for the adolescent.

Ebata (1990) further argued that adolescents may be at particular risk for stress-related problems because they have not yet developed fully mature cognitive, coping, and problem-solving skills needed to successfully adapt to stressful life events. It's highly probable that many murders occur because in addition to all of the other negative variables, the adolescent lacks impulse control, cognition, and often moral reasoning. When anyone is under a great deal of stress, it's easy to become irritable, angry, short-tempered, indecisive, and unpredictable.

Stern (1990) states that an important external stress mediator is the availability of social resources and supports. In many instances, the at-risk African American adolescent is unaware of the many resources that can be accessed.

A survey of seventy-nine of America's largest cities found that 249,324 gang members in 4,881 gangs committed 46,359 crimes and 1,072 homicides (Curry, et al., 1994). In the 1990s, there was an increase in gang-related crimes such as drive-by shootings, drug deals, retaliations, and homicides. In today's climate, it is unsafe for many children to walk through their neighborhoods wearing the wrong clothes. Many adolescents have also been murdered senselessly because someone wanted their jacket or their shoes.

Curry (et al., 1994) states that law enforcement officials define a "gang" as "an organized group with a recognized leader whose activities are either criminal or at the very least, threatening to the community." Many gangs in the inner city are well-established with a chain of command

and established rank. Many inner-city kids join gangs for a multitude of reasons: (1) to belong to something, (2) to identify with something, (3) because they feel it is glamorous, (4) to sell drugs, (5) to make money, (6) for protection, (7) for sex, (8) for power and status and because of the lack of guidance, nurturance, and discipline.

Gang activity does not stop on the streets. When adolescents are incarcerated, their gang mentality and their gang affiliation go with them. In many cases, gang members can still control the streets from behind bars. Behrend (1995) found a positive correlation between gang membership and homicidal behavior in African American adolescents. When looking at inner-city adolescent gangs and homicides, one has to utilize the multivariate approach because a multitude of negative factors are at play whenever an adolescent joins a gang. Recently, gangs have started to control the drug trade, and this factor alone has caused an escalation in the homicide rate of the inner-city African American male.

Since drugs are easily accessible to the inner-city adolescent gang member, one must also consider how these very same drugs might impair, cognitively and emotionally, an already emotionally impaired individual who is fragile and tenuous in spite of his false machismo.

SUMMARY

Upon reviewing the literature surrounding self-esteem, self-concept, and self-hatred, the results are consistent in that these psychological variables do contribute to the escalating African American male adolescent homicide rate. These psychological variables do impact the adolescent's behavior and increase his predilection to commit a homicide.

The variables described in this research take into consideration, stress, depression, family dynamics, gangs and drugs, racism, discrimination, and prejudice. All of these components can be categorized under either self-esteem, self-concept, or self-hatred.

The research shows that because there is a decrease in self-esteem, an alteration in self-concept, and a tendency toward self-hatred, there is also a tendency for the adolescent to view his future as being bleak, which in turn sets him on a course of self-destruction as well as a disregard for others who look like him and a disregard for the rules of society.

The research further suggests that the adolescent acts the way society expects him to act, and by doing so, carries through with the script that has been assigned him by the majority of society, his community, and his parents.

The theses being examined here are that all of the aforementioned intertwining variables coalesce to increase the vulnerability of the adolescent as far as homicides are concerned. These theories may be more anecdotal than empirical, but the research consistently shows that the adolescent is negatively affected by his environment and when he is negatively appraised by others.

According to George Mead, the self is formed through the individual's interaction with other members of society such as his peers, parents, teachers, and other agents of socialization.

The research also addresses the historical and contemporary forces that combine to produce a violent counterculture within this population. Many researchers dismiss the historical significance of racism, discrimination, and prejudice when addressing the African American adolescent male homicide rate. This research does take into consideration the profound significance of history as it relates to African Americans.

In the inner-city African American adolescent male population, often violence is seen as an acceptable form of behavior when resolving conflict Being socialized in a harsh and negative environment can also cause the adolescent to respond in a harsh and negative manner. This research explores the African American experience as it relates to being victimized in a society because of skin color. This research further looks at intervention strategies that can be utilized by clinicians when working with this population. It also addresses intervention strategies that can be put in place by policy makers.

The research also addresses the need to be loved by others. When this need is not met, the adolescent may tend to act out in anger and rage (Linehan, 1989). Much of the literature talks about maladaptive schemas that can be developed in childhood. This research focuses on such schemas and how they affect future behavior.

Self-hatred has been researched extensively for decades. This research also addresses self-hatred as an underlying cause of destructive behavior among inner-city African American adolescent males. Recent literature suggests that low self-concept based on skin color is no longer a problem among African American adolescent males (Bass, et al., 1982). This research contradicts these findings. Allen (1980) believes that those individuals who engage in self-hatred can easily project those feelings onto others who look like themselves. This research further examines the psyche of the inner-city African American male adolescent and how he engages in a broad spectrum of defense mechanisms when dealing with self-hatred due to racism, discrimination, and prejudice.

Research consistently shows that the homicide rate is highest among African American males (Center for Disease Control and Prevention, 1986). This research addresses this phenomenon along with the psychological variables that come into play.

Much attention has been paid to depression in the adolescent male, but not much significance has been placed on posturing and acting out behavior in this population. Paster (1985) has devoted a tremendous amount of time to this topic. This research fully addresses the depressogenic component and how it impacts the adolescent's decision to commit a homicide. The adolescent's environment is also taken into consideration. Durant (1994) found that depression was positively correlated with corporal punishment, family conflict, and exposure to violence.

The literature also addresses the absence of the father as it relates to homicides. The present study addresses the severity of this missing link in the life of the adolescent and how it impacts his behavior negatively.

Much attention has also been given to the role of the mother and the attachment or lack of attachment between her and the child. Winnicott (1954) did extensive research on the "good enough mother." This research addresses the importance of the mother and the father in the life of the child. This research further addresses the importance of the family as well as the responsibility that society has in protecting its children. Family organization is a crucial component in the psychological balance of any child, and the present study addresses these concerns. A strong family is a crucial component in the homicide puzzle. Society appears to be attempting to rebound from the "me" generation of the 1960s and 1970s. This research also focuses on the devastating effects of this aberration.

Alcohol and especially crack cocaine have been a deadly menace to the African American community. Much research has been done in this area, and this research further explores the devastating consequences of these drugs, especially as they relate to homicides.

Stress permeates all of society, but stress in the inner-city African American male is often overlooked. This crucial component has been critically analyzed in this study.

Gangs have also been around for quite some time. Presently, gangs are prevalent throughout America. Inner-city gangs are especially pervasive and many are dangerous. Kids join gangs for a variety of reasons, and this research explores the many reasons one would join a gang. Many gangs also control the flow of drugs, and this research explores this phenomenon as well as how it relates to homicides.

CHAPTER 2

AN EXPLORATION OF CONTRIBUTING PSYCHOLOGICAL VARIABLES

WHEN INVESTIGATING HOMICIDES among inner-city African American adolescent males, it is crucial to look at self-concept, self-esteem, and self-hatred.

SELF-CONCEPT, SELF-ESTEEM, AND THE SELF-HATRED CONCEPT

Before discussing these variables, it is important to examine the meaning of the word *self*. Sullivan (1971) states that the self is the content of consciousness at all times when one is thoroughly comfortable about one's self-respect, the prestige that one enjoys among one's fellows, and the respect and deference which they pay one. Sullivan further states that much of the praise and some of the blame that has come from parents, friends, teachers, and others with whom one has been significantly related have been organized into the content of the self. It is crucial to understand that Sullivan is saying that the person has a unique and individual perspective of the "self" in accordance to how he thinks society views him. In the case of the inner-city African American adolescent male, the self may be diminished because of society's negative view of him.

Sullivan also felt that anxiety is socially produced. He further states that individuals are made anxious by the conditions under which they live. He listed several anxiety-producing variables such as unemployment, intolerance, injustice, hostility, and many more. Inner-city African American males are confronted with all of these variables and more on a daily basis. Sullivan contends that by removing these variables or conditions, the wellsprings from which anxiety gushes will dry up.

As this research points out, the inner-city African American male can be destructive to the self and to those who are reflective of the self. Sullivan does not believe that humans are, by nature, destructive. He does believe that individuals may become destructive when their basic needs are frustrated. It is also important to understand that each individual is unique and that emphasis must be placed on the creative self and individualism. This is important when looking at inner-city African American adolescents who do not commit homicides. These individuals may be able to maintain a cohesive and healthy self because of a decrease in tension and anxiety due to consistent nurturance and caring during the developmental years and beyond.

Sullivan (1964) talks about the "bad me" and the "good me." He states that the "good me" personification results in interpersonal experiences that are rewarding in character. According to Sullivan, this starts in infancy and continues. It makes sense that if the person feels good about who he is, a healthy self is developed. The "bad me" arouses anxiety and will probably cause the self to be distorted and injured psychologically. The inner-city African American adolescent male may develop a personification or an image of himself that grows out of experiences with need satisfaction and anxiety.

According to Sullivan, the individual also develops an image of those around him. The inner-city African American adolescent male may make an appraisal of his reflected self, another African American male, and this may further arouse anxiety and anger. His negative appraisal may also further erode his self-esteem, alter his self-concept, and deepen his self-hatred to the point where it becomes easy for him to commit a murder against his mirror image, another African American adolescent.

SELF-CONCEPT

The Dictionary of Psychology (1985) defines self-concept as "one's concept of oneself in as complete and thorough a description as is possible for one to give." Terrell (1975) states that one explanation of delinquency and especially black-on-black homicides is that the individual lacks a positive self-concept. He further stated that those adolescents who have a low opinion of themselves compensate for their social inadequacy by resorting to antisocial behavior. Even though many of these adolescents may not yet be eighteen years of age, which qualifies them to be diagnosed with an antisocial disorder, they often do have a pervasive pattern of disregard for others.

When these adolescents are questioned about their homicidal behavior, they will often report that no one cares about them, so why should they care about anyone else? Others will talk about how they murdered their victim in the same vein in which a fisherman or a hunter boasts about his trophy. One can see that the individual has a skewed or negative concept of himself and a negative concept of what his relationship should be to others around him.

Spencer (1988) defines self-concept as "an individual's awareness of his or her own characteristics and attributes and the ways in which he or she is both like and unlike others."

According to Spencer (1988), identity formation is a process whereby children gain knowledge of such matters as their name, race, sex roles, social class, and the meanings these descriptions have for their lives. She further states that even though children may not understand the reasons that underlie these ascriptive meanings, these meanings evolve in the context of the specific culture to which the child belongs. Young children are quick to realize that they and their families are not welcomed in certain situations solely as a function of their race. Inner-city African American adolescent males are quick to pick up on these cues.

Because of this rejection or feeling of rejection, these adolescents may engage in negative behavior. It may even be possible that these negative feelings start in the early grades. Many of these adolescents may even be confused because they don't understand why they're discriminated against because of their race. This in itself can possibly cause self-contempt and contempt of others who resemble the "self." Spencer posits that these negative self-images can persist across a lifetime. It makes sense that if this theory holds true, these feelings can be transgenerational in that children can act out and possess the feelings of their parents, be they positive or negative.

Over the decades, much research has been done on the African American family. Banks (1976) found that young, preschool African American children generally evaluated the color black and black persons in a negative fashion. On the other hand, they tended to identify with Caucasian-type attributes. By the time these kids reach adolescence, these feelings and their worldview have been deeply formulated or ingrained. It is paramount that African American families remain strong so as to buffer the effects of a society that devalues some of its citizens. When this occurs, inner-city African American males will probably place more value on the lives of those who look like them.

THE STRESS-RELATED COMPONENT

Selye (1956), the grandfather of the stress theory, defines stress as any situation that causes the organism to adapt. He also talks about eustress and distress. Eustress is good stress or stress that is good for you, and distress is bad stress or stress that can cause a potential destructive response.

Stress in the inner-city African American male is a psychosocial variable that may be a crucial part of the puzzle in decreasing the inner-city African American male homicide rate. Stress does not take over when the individual becomes an adolescent, but it is insidious and can often start early in life.

Ebata (1990) stated that exposing an adolescent to stress in the home and his neighborhood causes the adolescent to become extremely vulnerable from a psychological standpoint.

At a correctional facility, one inner-city African American male talked about the relationship that he had with his mother. In his case, the father was absent. This adolescent portrayed his mother as a disciplinarian who had no regard for his feelings. According to the adolescent, his mother always said negative things about him, and instead of asking him to wash the dishes, she would tell him in an abrasive and condescending manner. When she was drinking, she would even invite her son to fight her. He further stated that he walked around mad all of the time. As he got older, this buildup of stress, tension, and anger caused him to abuse his girlfriend to the point where her face was swollen. This was a situation where the individual was trying to get his girlfriend to respect him just as his mother was demanding his respect. Moreover, he would never attack his mother, but his girlfriend was a substitute for the mother.

In the case of this adolescent, his mother was struggling to make ends meet. It is a well-known fact that economic depression and unemployment are related to many social problems impacting children (Toomey, 1990). According to Toomey, the family acts as a buffer for children. If the buffer is not there, it reduces the protection for the child.

Kasi and Cobb (1967) studied children reared in economic hardship. Their findings revealed that the parents had poor self-images and were insecure, less affectionate, and less responsive to their children. Kasl's and Cobb's belief is that this causes the children to feel rejected. This feeling of rejection can often times turn into anger and rage and a plethora of psychological symptoms.

Gibbs (1984) posited that African American children have always carried the brunt of poverty and economic hardship in America and are more at risk for experiencing a broad spectrum of sociological as well as psychological problems. Moreover, psychological distress in the parent can cause frustration and aggression in the adolescent (Gecas, 1979). More importantly, in many innercity African American homes, the father is absent, and this causes a tremendous amount of stress for the mother who is trying to hold together a family that is already teetering on the edge.

McLeyd (1990) believes that lower life status adversely affects the parent's psychological state. This may be true in many instances, but in many other instances, these fragile families manage to remain cohesive and survive. Many of the families that fall victim to psychological distress may also end up with adolescents who are antisocial and aggressive (Patterson, 1986). Patterson believes that antisocial and aggressive behavior is irritable and erratic. One would also think that if the parent's behavior was irritable and erratic, the child or adolescent would also take on the same characteristics. When stress is overwhelming in any individual, it can cause one to become very irritable. This irritability may also cause one to become very impulsive and engage in poor judgment, thus setting the stage to becoming a perpetrator of a homicide.

Gibbs (1984) stated that African American youth in modern American society could be described as an endangered species. Many innercity schools have written them off as uneducable, the juvenile system has been unsuccessful in teaching them, the mental health system has for the most part ignored them, and the social welfare system has not responded to their needs and seems to be ill-equipped to handle such a tremendous caseload. Society at large has also written these youth off because they are seen as deviant and do not meet the standards of mainstream society.

The inner-city African American male is highly misunderstood and ultimately rejected. When one is rejected, it also causes a great deal of chaos and confusion. This in turn can cause a great deal of stress in one's life. If the inner-city African American male is unable to navigate his way through the rough terrain of modem society, he is left behind to negotiate his way through a web of dysfunctionality and chaos whereby he has to pay a tremendous emotional price.

Myers and King (1980) stated that the mental health problems of the inner-city African American adolescent male result from the peculiar relationships between these youth and the system of social and economic relationships of which they are a part. Myers also believes that many of their difficulties can be viewed as the predictable products of efforts to adapt to oppressive social processes that result in the "manufacture of illness, disability, and social marginality." If the adolescent feels that he is not part of the mainstream culture, he sets up his own codes of behavior.

Information from the National Institute of Mental Health cited in Myers and King (1980) reveals that there has been an increase in psychiatric services for persons under the age of eighteen. Moreover, Myers and King also report that the rate of admission for youth under the age of fifteen per 100,000 population revealed that nonwhite youth are hospitalized for psychiatric disturbances at almost three times the rate of white youth in New York hospitals. The findings also suggest that the nonwhite patients have more severe disorders and more conduct and socialization disorders. Moreover, African American males were six times more likely than whites to have a diagnosis of schizophrenia and related disorders.

It is possible that inner-city African American adolescent males express their symptoms through acting out behaviors. This may in turn bring them to the police and the criminal justice system.

If many of these youth were treated early on, their symptoms would not escalate to the point where they would totally lose control and perpetrate a homicide. Myers and King (1980) believe there is a perception by many that a variety of behaviors of inner-city youth, which would be considered clinically meaningful in whites, are thought to be normal behavior for the inner-city adolescent youth and are not true psychiatric disorders. Lopez (1983) suggests that such a perception might cause one to under-pathologize. He calls this "under-pathologizing bias." It is extremely important to be able to intervene early on so that the mental health problem of the adolescent does not deteriorate into an intractable disability.

Likewise, Banks (1976) believes that many of the behaviors expressed by inner-city African American males, such as anger, suspiciousness, and challenges to authority may be healthy and appropriate responses to the day-to-day insults to the ego of the inner-city African American adolescent. This may indeed be a useful coping strategy for the inner-city African American adolescent.

Myers and King (1980) believe that the adolescent male is at a higher risk for a variety of illnesses, disabilities, injuries, socioemotional maladjustments, and death than most other American youth. They further believe that the inner-city African American youth has to confront both normal and extraordinary developmental tasks. Because of these inequities, the inner-city African American adolescents are being devastated. Meyers and King (1980) state that there is a deep structure coterminous with the capitalistic social order that maintains these social conditions. What they are referring to is long-standing economic and social exploitation that is designed to benefit a few. Meyers and King also believe that the inner-city adolescent interacts with these conditions, changes, and is changed by these conditions. They label the influence of this larger social context, if you will, a social stress condition.

Myers (1982) proposed the "urban stress model" as one explanation for the behavior of the inner-city African American male. His theory draws upon the social stress and its effect.

The basic paradigm of his model consists of Selye's (1956) and Lazarus's and Folkman's (1967, 1974) stress adaptation models, which propose adaptation as a precursor to disease and system malfunctions.

Several empirically validated assumptions are made in this model. Lazarus and Folkman (1982) stated that the greater the amount, intensity, duration, and meaningfulness of the stress experienced, the greater the likelihood of illness and the greater the severity of the resultant disorder.

Dohrenwend and Dohrenwend (1970) and Meyers (1982) posit that the negative interaction of two factors, race and social class, serves to create a cross-generational pattern of stress induction and stress accumulation in the African American poor. Brenner (1984) posits that this pattern is created by the cumulative effect of greater exigencies of daily living and greater risks of facing troubles that place increasing demands on already taxed resources. It makes sense that if the African American adult is overwhelmed by stress, the child or adolescent will adapt the same behavior.

In contemporary society, the homicide rate in the African American community has reached epidemic levels, and this may be an indication that the inner-city African American adolescent male may be less able to cope with his surroundings than previous generations. He may also be functioning under a tremendous amount of stress. He may even be psychologically primed to perceive and react to stimuli as more stressful than whites would.

Watts (1978) believes that children in insidiously stressful poverty environments may even begin to develop in utero, significantly increasing risks for a number of disorders. This is an extremely important area that needs to be studied further.

When looking at the stress component, one must also look at the positive attributes considered typical of the African American community. This includes the social networks such as the extended family and the church, which have historically served as sources of support to mediate stressors and to provide a foundation for survival and upward mobility. Myers (1980) believes that the social networks and the resources of the traditional African American family and community have been undermined by desertion, substance abuse, and individualism and have become less effective in fulfilling their buffering function.

Many of these inner-city adolescents are very narcissistic and hedonistic and will say such things as, "I want it all for me and I don't care about anybody else." Many will reject the church, which is a fortress in the African American community. Moreover, they will often totally reject the rules of society. If the rules are stacked against them, there is no reason for them to comply with the rules as they perceive it. If their parents or other adults can't cope effectively, neither can they. Many are also unable to problem-solve or read situations accurately.

Myers (1980) also believes that poor inner-city African American adolescent males are highly stress-vulnerable because of mediating external stress-inducing factors but also because of internal factors that may reduce their stress-coping effectiveness. He also sees the latter as part of the legacy of oppression and racism.

He further states that they are still being reinforced by the social processes that condemn many African American youth to a condition of social marginality. Examples or social marginality are class oppression, the remediation or mentality in education, the graduation of functional illiterates, the proliferation of drugs, and the increasing tendency to use violence as the solution to interpersonal conflicts.

Ilfeld (1978) believes that stress in the everyday life of the poor inner-city African American male is insidious and pervasive. The insidiousness of the stress is what makes it so dangerous. Usually, it is out of control before anything can be done about it.

Many inner-city adolescent males use alcohol and marijuana to cope with everyday life. This can be a deadly combination because the drugs can further cloud the judgment of a youth whose judgment in many cases is already impaired. All too often, the result of poor judgment can lead to a homicide.

One must also look at historical perspectives when looking at how the inner-city African American male adolescent handles stress. If one develops a schema early on that is maladaptive, that schema will follow him across time. By the time the inner-city African American male has become an adolescent, he has been habituated to act and react in certain ways when confronted or aroused. His maladaptive behavior can be changed, but he needs to be shown that his previous behaviors were indeed maladaptive.

An adolescent at a correctional facility once discussed how another adolescent pushed and elbowed him while he stood in line at a movie theater, waiting to buy popcorn. This altercation caused a fight to ensue between the perpetrator of the altercation and the other adolescent who was pushed. First, the perpetrator did not say, "Excuse me" as he forced his way to the front or the line. His style or relating to others in a harsh and negative manner had been developed early on. Likewise, the victim of this inconsiderate and abrasive act responded in a manner that he was accustomed to.

All too often, the inner-city African American male will react to a perceived threat in this manner because to him, this ensures that his respect will remain intact. More importantly, these negative patterns or behaviors are an integral part of his coping mechanisms that may have been established in early childhood. Jenkins and Bell (1991) state that a large number of inner-city children are exposed to violence on a regular basis. This being true, the inner-city African American male may become immune or numb to the effects of violence and particularly homicides. Many African American male adolescents will boast about committing a violent act or a homicide. They will often say that if they don't know the victim, there is no reason to be sad. Likewise, if they know a victim of a homicide, many will profess to be sad for one or two days, but then it's business as usual, and they continue their routinized behavior. It appears that many of these adolescents adapt to a hostile and noxious environment. Even though adaptation may take place, the effects of violence may be underestimated.

Pynoos and Eth (1985) suggest that repeated violent acts, which can include homicides, can seriously deplete a child's inner resources. Terr (1989) believes that repeated traumas may lead to anger, despair, and severe psychic numbing that can result in major personality changes.

Jenkins and Bell (1991) believe that exposure to violence can have serious consequences as it relates to the mental health of the adolescent. They further state that the adolescent's dysfunctional behavior can manifest itself in the form of poor achievement, acting out, and many other negative behaviors.

Another significant variable to be scrutinized when looking at the lives of these adolescents is the issue of abandonment or loss. Humphrey (1987) believes that this may be an extremely important variable. Many inner-city African American males who are incarcerated for committing a homicide have experienced tremendous losses through emotional or physical abandonment of one or both parents. In many cases, one or both parents have been addicted to alcohol or crack cocaine, which prevents them from providing adequate nurturance. The adolescent may try to cope with this anomaly as best as he knows how, but the anger and the rage are insidious, and an eruption can occur in the form of a homicide during the adolescent years. These higher levels of stress early in life can put the adolescent in a position of high vulnerability of becoming a perpetrator of a homicide.

THE DEPRESSOGENIC COMPONENT

According to DSM-IV (APA, 1994), depression is classified as an affective disorder characterized by depressed mood, irritability, marked diminished interests or pleasure in all or almost all activities most of the day, a significant weight loss or weight gain, a decrease or increase in appetite, insomnia or hypersomnia nearly every day, psychomotor agitation nearly every day, fatigue or loss of energy, worthlessness, guilt, lack of concentration, and recurrent thoughts of suicide or death. DSM-IV further describes the depression of adolescent boys as manifested by negativism, antisocial behavior, feelings of wanting to leave home, of not being understood or approved of, restlessness, grouchiness, aggression, school difficulties, withdrawal, and drug abuse.

When one thinks of depression, what generally comes to mind is all of the negative symptoms that would cause an individual to become withdrawn, lethargic, and listless. It is also important to take into consideration that depression can often be masked by aggressive, flamboyant, and acting-out behaviors. For the inner-city adolescent male who commits a homicide, this may be an important variable that is often overlooked. Among these youths are those who are depressed and who may be acting out because of their depression. Moreover, acting out may be a cry for help.

Gibbs (1984) recently urged that the highest priority be given to the inner-city African American male adolescent. Statistics show that African American males are two-and-a-half times more likely to be victims of crime and seven times more likely to be murdered (US Bureau of Census, 1980).

Many inner-city African American males are from a single-parent household that is often headed by a female. In many instances, these adolescents are referred to as the underclass, and many people in society have written them off as thugs, failures, drug dealers, and criminals. These adolescents will often reject the rules of society, and society will often be just as rejecting of them. Many of them give up because they feel that whatever they do, society will reject them. Moreover, they care about no one because no one cares about them. Because many of the fathers don't claim paternity, these adolescents feel angry, frustrated, isolated, alienated, abandoned, and rejected. In many instances, the already overtaxed mother has the awesome chore of raising adolescent males who are out of control and practically raising themselves.

Blos (1972) states that the adolescent transitional phase in itself is disruptive. He goes on to say that the adolescent is searching for identity and social independence, which contributes to the turbulence. He further states that there is a sense of helplessness, inadequacy, and failure.

Paster (1985) posits that many variables intertwine to perpetuate the plight of the inner-city African American adolescent male. She stated that these variables are political, societal, economic, interpersonal, and intrapsychic. In addition to being intertwined, these variables are reciprocally reinforcing. Many politicians take the position that if you build more prisons, they will come. Others take the position that these adolescents are the products of drug-abusing parents and that there is no hope for them. Early intervention has been ruled out, and instead, a punitive stance has been adopted. If there wasn't a need for a penal system, judges, attorneys, public defenders, correctional officers, police officers, social workers, and many others would be unemployed. So as one can clearly see, there is a feedback system that is often lucrative in nature for many people.

Society feels quite safe when these adolescents are behind bars. Many take the position that once they're locked up, the key should be thrown away. From an intrapsychic standpoint, the seed for becoming aggressive was probably planted in the adolescent at an early age. Society has rejected him and written him off, and those close to him have reminded him of how bad he is and that he will never amount to anything. These early schemas can lead to depressive symptoms in adolescence.

Even though the inner-city African American adolescent may swagger and engage in a great deal of posturing and flamboyance, he may also feel a sense of helplessness, inadequacy, and failure. He may also feel worthless and that he is a nothing (Giovacchini, 1977). These issues may also be more intimidating to adolescents because their sense of powerlessness is reinforced by poverty and discrimination (Paster, 1985).

Many of these adolescents will also purchase expensive jewelry, clothing, and other items that will help them deal with the deadness and the depression. Their ability to impress others gives them a sense of power and status.

Akhtar (1983) posits that the adolescent's narcissism reduces his ability to differentiate between impulse, thought, and action. He expresses this in the form of inconsistent control, inconsistent judgment, and acting out behavior. It also appears that the adolescent may also have a tremendous amount of self-contempt, which could manifest itself in the form of unreliable controls and inconsistent judgment.

Most adolescents are concerned about morphology or body form. If he is poor, African American, and unacculturated, he may see himself as someone to be feared because this is what the world at large has told him (Paster, 1985). If the adolescent devalues his own life, there is not much hope that he will value anyone else's life. The person that he commits a homicide against may be a mirror image of himself. Furthermore, he may see his peers on the street as also being inadequate, hopeless, angry, contemptuous, and frustrated.

Paster (1985) believes that many of these adolescents would rather live in the fantasy world of their childhood, but instead, they are forced to deal with a harsher reality. Many of them long for their missing father who has never played a part in their lives. The paternal abandonment may have generated a feeling of loss in some of these adolescents, and in turn, a schema could have been developed that led to depressive tendencies. It is a well-known fact that in cases of unresolved grief, depression can occur.

Paster (1985) believes that most inner-city adolescents do come through this stage unscathed. They function adequately, they are hopeful, and they do grow into responsible adults. Others, she feels, become casualties. These are the ones who are depressed and act out. Paster (1985) also believes that because many of these adolescents act in a flamboyant manner, combined with their age, their race, and their socioeconomic status, the underlying depressed state of the adolescent may go unnoticed. Carlson and Cantell (1980) posit that depression is an affective disorder that can manifest itself in the form of dysphoria, disturbance in appetite or sleep, change in weight, psychomotor agitation or retardation, decreased energy, guilt, feelings of worthlessness, difficulty concentrating, and thoughts of death and suicide.

It's unfortunate, but many inner-city African American adolescents do not have the luxury of receiving any kind of psychiatric intervention to deal with depressive symptoms or any other psychological disorder unless it is on an emergency basis. If the youth is depressed, it goes unnoticed because clinicians as well as others expect the inner-city adolescent to act in a certain manner: Negative behavior is expected of him because of cultural predilections. Shanok (1983) posits that violent behavior transforms the adolescent into a larger and more frightening person so that the social pathology and not the psychological pathology is recognized.

Lewis (1979) concludes from her study that disturbed African American adolescents were diagnosed into a correctional setting when they should have been diagnosed into a mental health setting. Again, their behavior was seen as culturally appropriate.

It is paramount that clinicians examine their own cultural biases when dealing with this misunderstood population. Paster (1985) cautions that many times, therapists and many others in positions of responsibility and authority see these individuals as angry, dangerous, inaccessible, and quite different. In many instances, these variables as well as the complexity of their masks get in the way of understanding them. This also limits adequate care. It is also possible that mental health workers as well as others in the community are so preoccupied with the flamboyance that the depression is totally missed. Paster also believes that psychological batteries, social histories, diagnostic interviews, and physical examinations should be administered. She goes on to say that these investigative tools should be given and assessed with the least amount of preconception. Her main premise is that if this is done, it will not only tease out the anger but the sadness, the sense of worthlessness, and the hopelessness.

It has been reported by many inner-city adolescents that they feel a sense of deadness. It would make sense that in order to relieve this sense of deadness, they would engage in risky behaviors that would include guns and violence. It is also easy for them to use these guns because in many cases, they take the position that "It's them or me." It is also common to hear many of them say, "We all have to die sooner or later."

Because of the deadness in their lives, many of them don't mind dying sooner than later. To them, their lives have been so disappointing and so negative that death is often welcomed. Paster (1985) takes the position that the depressed inner-city African American male may engage in flamboyant overactivity to divert his attention away from his passivity and sense of deadness.

It is extremely difficult to know the impact that masked depression has on the African American male homicide rate, but further research should be done to identify the significance of this important variable.

Durant (et al., 1995), found that adolescents who felt that there was little chance that they would live to be twenty-five years of age had higher depression-scale scores. When social supports are almost nonexistent, depression appears to be an undesirable consequence according to Durant. It would seem that if the inner-city African American adolescent male has a sense of hopelessness, his depression would also increase exponentially.

Abramson (et al., 1978) talks about the "hopelessness theory of depression." This theory hypothesizes the existence of an as yet unidentified subtype of depression-hopelessness depression. What this means is that there is a sequence of events in a causal chain, beginning with a negative life event that culminates in hopelessness and depression. For many inner-city adolescents today, negative events are commonplace and in many instances are becoming unavoidable.

Seligman (1975) engaged in laboratory experiments with animals to test his theory of learned helplessness. In his study, animals did not try to get away from the shock after struggling initially. After a while, they simply lay passively and endured the shock. After a while, they learned to be helpless.

The inner-city African American adolescent male is often confronted with a volley of negative life experiences that culminate into depressogenic symptoms. These symptoms can cause him to become very volatile with homicidal behavior as the end result. The depressogenic component is a very important variable that needs to be given grave consideration when working with this population.

In essence, the masked depression that many inner-city African American adolescent males exhibit may manifest itself in extreme aggressivity.

Boone (1990) studied aggression in adolescent African American males. His results demonstrated that if the mother was prone to express love toward the adolescent through emotional and psychological support, the adolescent demonstrated nonaggressive tendencies. This is an important variable because in many instances, the adolescent who commits a homicide does not receive the love and nurturance needed to maintain a sense of psychological balance. Many perpetrators of a homicide have been often physically and emotionally abused all of their lives. Love and discipline go hand in hand, and when they're absent, the adolescent is at risk for becoming engaged in negative or criminal behavior.

Boone also found that when the adolescent engaged in regular church attendance with the parent, he did not engage in aggressive acts of violence. This variable is crucial because regular church attendance, according to Boone, is characterized by self-respect and concern for others. The church in the African American community has always been a fortress and a vital part of the African American community. It is important to note that inner-city African American males who do not commit homicides have consistent love and discipline and a sense of right and wrong instilled in them by their parent or parents as well as moral and religious teachings. Many people may feel that two parents are needed in order for these adolescents to successfully navigate their way through the chaos that surrounds them in a nonaggressive fashion. Emotional and psychological support by one parent is sufficient in bringing about a sense of balance in the life of the adolescent.

Many mothers will try to satiate and appease their sons by giving them material things. From the mother's perspective, this is how she shows love and affection toward her son. Many adolescents who are incarcerated will report that their mothers gave them everything they wanted. This did not prevent them from being aggressive because the love and nurturance were not there. In many families, where the adolescent is nonaggressive, both the mother and the father are cohesive in the way in which they discipline the adolescent. When the adolescent gets one clear message from both parents, he will generally respond positively when disciplined. If he senses ambiguity and fragmentation in the parental relationship, then he will test the limits of the parents.

Rutter (1984) reports that the mothers' attitude toward their sons might be important for the development of aggressive habits. In the case of the adolescent murderer, the mother may be contributing to his delinquency by her unaffectionate actions as well as condoning much of his negative behavior.

Boone (1990) found that adolescents who tend to be nonaggressive were consistently reprimanded by their mothers in the form of physical force, forceful verbal discipline, and the loss of privileges and other pleasurable experiences for undesirable behaviors than were adolescents who show aggressive behaviors. When mothers are too lax and inconsistent in their disciplinary practices, the end result is aggressivity. Boone also looked at the father-son dyad. He reported that the mother-son dyad is a much more powerful predictor of aggression in boys. In many instances, the father of the inner-city adolescent male is not around. The mothers want to love and protect their sons, but at the same time, it is important for them to recognize that their parenting style is a contributing factor to later aggressive behavior in their sons.

Boone (1990) also posits that high levels of intrafamily aggression and conflict and strained communication by family members also carry over into the community. The adolescent has not been able to resolve interpersonal conflict in the home, and this attributional style follows him wherever he goes.

Weiner (et al., 1982) found that anger is experienced when an individual holds another person responsible for the negative or harmful consequences of a social transaction. If one feels threatened, attributing blame to someone else may serve as a defensive coping strategy that fuels anger arousal and increases the chances that one will respond in an aggressive manner. This may be particularly true among impulsive, under-socialized adolescents. The under-socialized adolescent may be quick to anger because he has misinterpreted environmental cues.

Fondacaro and Heller (1990) state that the adolescent tends to attribute blame for problems in ambiguous interactions to global dispositional characteristics of others. This may have to do with social cognitive skills.

Dodge (1981) found that aggressive boys made causal inferences more quickly and paid less attention to available social cues than nonaggressive boys did. Dodge is saying that aggressive boys may inaccurately appraise their transactions with their peers. As a result, they may select incompetent response strategies based on these biased perceptions.

Winnicott (1967) posits that deprivation early on causes antisocial behavior and aggression. Winnicott believes that a child can go through life with certain distortions of reality testing. When looking at the inner-city African American adolescent male, one can plainly see this distortion in reality as it relates to his decision-making and problem-solving abilities. Winnicott further believes that the child learns early on that it is safe to be aggressive and have aggressive feelings because of the framework of the family representing society in a localized fashion. In other words, the aggressivity that is learned in the family is carried over into society.

Morton (1967) believes that aggression is acquired. The innercity adolescent who engages in aggressive behavior has not only learned this behavior in the home but is inundated with aggressivity in his environment.

Klein (1986) paid close attention to the superego. She posited that the superego developed independently of biological influences and was heavily influenced by the nature of the child's relationship with the parents and the problems of the primary instincts. She paid particular attention to the processes of introjection and projection. These, she says, are derived from the drives and their interactions with the primary objects of the child's early experience.

Again, one can clearly see that aggression is learned from early on. Bowlby (1979) posits that aggression occurs because of failure to attach during the early years in a child's life. In many cases, there is a severe disruption of attachment with the caregiver. For the innercity African American male, the mother-son dyad is one that is tenuous and can cause antisocial behavior and extreme aggression if attachment is disrupted. This also holds true for the father. When the father is absent, the child is deprived of a strong and stable love object he so desperately needs to help him negotiate the social order in which he finds himself. Thus, the child is unable to view the world as a nurturing environment.

Spitz (1950) believes the child is therefore unable to form identifications. If there is no identification, the child will more than likely not be able to identify with other human beings. This may partially explain why it is so easy for the inner-city African American male to commit a homicide.

Freud (1953–1964) stated that the aim of aggression is destruction. More importantly, he stated that this destruction is turned outward. In the case of the inner-city African American male, this destruction is turned onto someone who is a mirror image of himself.

SELF-ESTEEM

Self-esteem is another area that is controversial. Webster's Dictionary of Psychology (1985) defines self-esteem as "the degree to which one values oneself." Many empirical studies show that African Americans have self-esteem equal to or greater than that of whites (Gordon, 1969). Rosenberg (1970) posits that a person's self-esteem is a product of how that person believes others see him. He is suggesting that persons belonging to low-status groups will internalize the negative evaluation of society and therefore have low self-esteem. Festinger (1954) posits that self-esteem is, in part, a consequence of individuals comparing themselves with others and making negative self-evaluations. His premise also states that if African Americans experience low levels of social and economic achievement in American society and recognize their status in comparison with whites, this may lead to low self-esteem.

It's also possible that inner-city African American males may watch the hopes and dreams of their parents and other adults become shattered, and in turn, their own self-esteem is shattered. Many innercity adolescents repeatedly say that they will not live to be twenty-one years of age. Their outlook on life is often bleak and hopeless, and in many cases, this may also correlate with their level of self-esteem.

Rosenberg (1979) states that self-esteem is strongly correlated to the reflected appraisals of parents, friends, and teachers. In many instances, teachers expect the adolescent to fail, parents give many negative messages to the adolescent, and the adolescent emulates the negative behavior and the negative self-images of his peers. It's highly possible that what is produced from these messages are anger, rage, and destructiveness on the part of the adolescent. Moreover, the more society engages in benign neglect, the more the adolescent continues on his destructive path.

Griffin (1991) posits that humiliation erodes self-esteem. He further states that this humiliation starts early in life. The damage from this humiliation also starts early in life.

In the city of Milwaukee, Wisconsin, possession of small amounts of marijuana was recently reduced to a misdemeanor because a high number of African American adolescent males were being sent to jail or prison for possession of marijuana while white adolescents in the suburbs were given small fines (*Milwaukee Journal*, 1998). This inequity further reinforces the negative feelings African American adolescent males may have about their value as American citizens. This type of blatant injustice can only increase the anger and rage of the African American adolescent male. When this happens on a daily basis, more than likely, the adolescent may consciously or unconsciously devalue the life of someone who looks like him because he and other African Americans are devalued. Since he is already full of anger and rage, taking the life of someone who is already devalued by society may be extremely easy for him.

FAMILY DYNAMICS

In capturing the total essence of the African American family, one must travel back in time to gain an appreciation of the strength and diversity of the African American family. Before being brought to America as slaves, African Americans belonged to various tribes from many African states. The legacy of this proud and rich history has been documented by many historians (e.g., Bohannan, 1964; Herskovits, 19858; Nobles, 1980).

In spite of attempts to diminish and denigrate the African American family, its strength and its resiliency have allowed it to survive through the centuries. In many African tribes, there existed an altruistic feature in that the primary concern was for the group, not the individual.

The African American family was also built on a strong religious foundation. Nobles (1980) stated that religion in the African tribes was an integral part of life. He further stated that "religion accompanied the individual from conception to long after his physical death." When one talks about the African American family, the institution of slavery has to be a salient feature to be examined because of the disruption that it caused. In an attempt to dominate and subjugate, slave-owners, without regard for the consequences, attempted to blatantly destroy the strong kinship connections as well as the culture that represented centuries of evolution. Moreover, the African American male was stripped of his dignity and self-respect.

There were also many other attempts made to destroy the African American family. Giddings (1984) gathered a great deal of research on the impact of slavery on the African American family. In his research, he found that traditional tribal marriages were not allowed and, just as sinister, slaves were not allowed to marry according to European customs. Giddings also discovered that since men and women could not legalize their marriages, no child born to a slave was seen as a family member. In the mind of the slave-owner, this legitimized his evil act. Any family member could be sold at will. Giddings (1984) also researched sexuality as it related to slaves. He found that both male and female slaves were abused sexually. The men were used as breeders to increase and sustain the labor supply, while women were used as sex objects to satiate the desires of the slave-owners.

In spite of deprivation of human rights and human dignity, African Americans still sought to adhere to family and spirituality. They also established their own marriage rituals and engaged in the process of informal adoptions when slaves were either killed or sold. According to Franklin-Boyd (1982), the kinship network still remains a major mechanism for coping with the strain of an oppressive society.

Jones (1980) challenged the deficit view of African American family life. During the 1960s and the 1970s, many scholars challenged the pathological theories of African American families. Moynihan (1965) stated that the African American family was pathological, disorganized, and chaotic. His analysis was skewed but nonetheless put into motion social policies that negatively affected African American families.

Franklin (1989) explored the strengths in well-functioning African American families. Even though many African American families are headed by women, Franklin believes it would be a mistake to view most African American families as inherently pathological. Dukes (1985) posits that a healthy single parent and a support network from an extended family can result in healthy family functioning.

This is also true for many inner-city African American families, but at the same time, these families are the most fragile and the most tenuous. In essence, the adolescent males in these families are the most likely to perpetrate a homicide and they are the most likely to be a victim of a homicide. In the absence of family stability, chaos and violence are often the tragic outcome.

In the 1960s, and particularly the 1970s, America was rebounding from the Vietnam War. Most African Americans were feeling confident that they would receive equity in a fair and just society. The "me" generation, if you will, was very hedonistic, and this contributed to the dissolution of not just African American families but many other families.

Starting in the 1960s, African American families made many gains socially and economically because of changes in civil rights laws, which allowed for upward mobility. In the research done by Franklin-Boyd (1982), it was found that 40 percent of all African Americans are considered to be in the middle class while 10 percent are considered to be in the upper class. On the other hand, 50 percent are considered to be in the lower class where there exists a tremendous amount of poverty and social ills. This is also the population with a tremendous amount of family dysfunctionality, and this is also the target population, the focus of this study.

The social and economic gains of the 1960s did not benefit a large segment of the African American population. In fact, even back in the 1960s, an alarm was sounded that family dissolution was reaching catastrophic proportions (Aaron, 1978). Since the 1960s, the divorce rate has soared, and this has further weakened the family.

In the 1940s, it was common for many girls to become pregnant in their teens, irrespective of race. The most blatant difference then was that the vast majority of these teenage girls married right away. The marriage bond also assured family stability. In 1980, 68 percent of births to African American women between the ages of fifteen to twenty-four were outside of marriage (Wilson, 1985). Today, this number still seems to be increasing. The women's liberation movement, which started in middle-class America, also seems to have filtered down to African American women as well. It also appears that African American women in the lower class are choosing to go it alone, rather than have a supportive male in their life.

This shift has caused a tremendous amount of confusion for the male because it has made him unsure of his role. This schism between males and females has also adversely affected the children because nurturance and discipline from the father are nonexistent. When love and discipline are provided, the child will more than likely not be as apt to be attracted to the negative things in his environment. As noted earlier, many homicides are committed because the adolescent is angry and full of rage. With a functional family setting, he may not act out in such a deviant manner.

Griggs (1968) posits that the father's absence could have a detrimental effect on children. Hartnagel (1970) states that his studies revealed that the self-concept of African American males was lowered when the father was absent. Many inner-city African American adolescents who enter the correctional system often express the anger they feel toward their fathers for not being there for them. One thirteen-year-old adolescent went so far as to say, "I never had anyone there to teach me the difference between right and wrong." Also, when many of these adolescents enter the correctional setting, they bring with them a tremendous amount of emotional baggage, and the family is usually in disarray. Their social skills are often very poor because they have had poor socialization in the home. Additionally, the mothers are struggling to maintain their health and their sanity in the face of tremendous odds. Moreover, it is common for the adolescent to have a brother, an uncle, or a father who is also incarcerated. Criminal activity and incarceration are seen as normal by him. With the advent of the crack cocaine epidemic, many of these families have been virtually destroyed. Also, many of these adolescents not only feel abandoned by the father but also feel emotionally abandoned by the mother because of her addiction to drugs or alcohol. It is also true that many of these mothers are exceptionally young and are overburdened with the responsibility of having to raise children without adequate parenting skills. These mothers also tend to have less educational and less work experience and less financial resources (Bell, 1968). These problems will become even more complicated as each individual state starts to dismantle welfare programs that have essentially contributed to family dysfunctionality because the system that has been in place for decades encouraged lethargy, helplessness, and hopelessness.

These programs also laid the groundwork for absentee fathers because welfare payments would be discontinued if an adult male were present in the home. It appears that the state government expected the African American women to be dependent and subservient while expecting the male to be either drug or alcohol-dependent or incarcerated. Not much has changed because the inner-city African American male is still expected to be incarcerated. This is evident by the number of prisons being built today.

Moynihan (1965) states that within the African American family, there exists a web of pathology. It appears that he is saying that this pathology is profound and intractable. With 50 percent of African Americans living below the poverty line, there is a tremendous amount of cause for alarm (Franklin-Boyd, 1982). FranklinBoyd also contend that women and children will be affected most by poverty.

When families are strong, it makes sense that the community will also be strong. In order for these families to become functional, many things have to change. The legacy of racism cannot be overlooked as an important variable that negatively affects family life.

Wilson (1987) posited a web of factors that contribute to the decay of the inner city and the breakdown of the African American family who resides there. He contends that the movement of the middle-class African American professionals and the exodus of a number of working-class African Americans from the inner city negatively affect the infrastructure of the inner city. What is left behind is an underclass of very poor African Americans with little or no job skills. When this phenomenon occurs, social problems are exacerbated (Wilson, 1987).

The dysfunctional family is on a lower rung of the economic and social ladder, and it is possible that the anger and rage are turned on one another. When the adolescent male commits a homicide, this gesture could be a symptom of a larger problem in the family and in the community. Whenever a child or an adolescent is brought in for family psychotherapy, he may be seen as a scapegoat or the identified patient when he is really trying to bring attention to a larger problem within the family. The perpetrator of a homicide acts out in a violent nature, and he may be overburdened from living in a chaotic family. In essence, he may even be the "identified patient." Early childhood intervention that puts the family first may change the lives of adolescents for the better.

President Bill Clinton talked about forming the new family covenant. It may be quite a long time before the traditional two-parent family is seen again. The top priority now should be to help bring stability to these fractured families that are, in most cases, femaleheaded. If the parents have no job skills and no money and live in an area with no job opportunities, it is extremely hard to exercise responsibility for the basic needs of their children. The problems that plague many inner-city families are extremely complex and will be difficult to solve, but a concerted effort must be made to bring this population into the mainstream so that they can also enjoy the fruits from a bountiful country. When this happens, poor inner-city African American adolescent males will feel good about themselves and there will be no need to take the life of someone who looks like himself.

GANGS AND DRUGS

The World Book Dictionary defines *gang* as "a group of people acting or going around together, especially a group engaged in some improper, unlawful or criminal activity." When most of the general public hears "gang" or "gang member," all kinds of negative images come to mind from drug dealing to destructive behavior to homicides.

Throughout American history, gangs have been a part of the American culture or subculture, if you will. During the prohibition period in this country, gangs were prevalent, and they were feared by many. There were multiple gangland-type murders and territorial wars like the ones that are sweeping the country today between youthful and adolescent gang members. This is a tragic epidemic that has caused tremendous concern and has devastated many African American communities. The psychological and economic costs have been staggering.

Community advocates and governmental agencies have attempted to curb the gang problem through various innovative programs, but gang involvement and gang recruitment continue to escalate in spite of diversionary tactics. As a matter of fact, gang members are being recruited at much earlier ages. It is not at all uncommon to hear an adolescent say that he was recruited into a gang at the age of eight or nine. When adolescents are indoctrinated into gangs, often they have to commit heinous crimes such as gang rape, armed robbery, battery, auto theft, home invasion, and murder. The inductee will many times have to take a brutal beating at the hands of other members of the gang.

Many inner-city African American adolescents join gangs for many reasons.

Kaplan (1975) states that "persons characterized by negative self-attitudes are motivated to adopt deviant response patterns…that are associated with the enhancement of self-attitudes." He further states that the negative behaviors displayed by gang members work to improve their self-attitudes. The adolescent does not get a great deal of positive feedback from those at home or from his teachers at school. As a matter of fact, many teachers view absences and lack of interest as prime reasons to divert the already troubled youth into special education classes. One adolescent further feels more degraded, humiliated, alienated, rejected, and confused.

Many inner-city African American adolescents state that they joined a gang because they wanted to belong to something. In all facets of society, people have a need to belong. Maslow (1967) talks about the need to belong, to be loved, to be safe, and to have a level of self-esteem. For psychologists, there is a need to belong to the American Psychological Association. Additionally, people have a need to belong to a church, mosque, temple, or synagogue. Others have a need to join the Kawanis Club, the Rotary Club, the Masons, or other affiliations.

Having membership in a chosen organization brings with it status and a high level of acceptance. When the inner-city African American male joins a gang, he is looking for the same type of self-actualization. Many inner-city adolescents will tell you that they also join the gang for safety reasons or for protection. Because many inner-city adolescents live in environments that are not safe; the gang to many of them can be a refuge and a safe haven.

Modeling is also a variable that comes into play in terms of the behaviors that are imitated by the younger inner-city male. Bandura (1969) talks about vicarious learning and vicarious reinforcement The inner-city adolescent will learn from his environment through watching those around him. The adolescent readily learns that there are consequences for his negative behavior, usually in the form of positive reinforcement from his peers he idolizes. In many cases, he has no father who is visible and who can give positive exan1ples to follow. He will therefore fill the void of the absent father with misdirected guidance from someone who can and will influence his behavior negatively.

Inner-city adolescents are also lured into gangs because of glamour, excitement, girls, and money. Many gang members have repeatedly said that they will not accept minimum wages working at fast-food restaurants or other establishments when they can make hundreds of dollars a day selling drugs. The idea of making fast money is one that especially lures these adolescents to the gang. Older gang members have been known to pay nine and ten-year-old males in excess of thirty dollars a day to be lookout persons for police officers or other suspicious-looking people who will possibly interfere with the drug trade.

Brantley and Dirosa (1994) state that a dysfunctional home life, plus sentiments of discontent, lack of respect for authority, and the effect of residing in a depressed housing area can be recruiting tools for gang members. These vulnerable youth are not doing well in school and are already on their way to dropping out.

Brantley and Dirosa (1994) did a recent study of African American gang members in Milwaukee, Wisconsin. Each gang member was interviewed, and it was found that each gang member had dropped out of school. Moreover, most of these adolescents had been expelled from school for fighting.

There is also a pattern involved in this type of delinquency. The first step is that the adolescent's grades will worsen, followed by expulsion, followed by multiple contacts with the police department, and finally juvenile corrections. It is not uncommon for every male in the family to be a gang member. Brantley and Dirosa (1994) state that because gang members have made such an impact in the social fabric of the inner cities, recruiting is especially easy. Gangs have also proliferated to the point where there is a great deal of divisiveness. In talking to several gang members, it was learned that there are several branches of the Vice-Lords as well as several branches of the gangster Disciples and other gangs. These offshoots are another way for the gang members to distinguish themselves as being different.

The gang problem today is not just a problem in the large metropolitan areas. There is a growing concern that the problem is escalating in smaller cities as well for the same reasons that have been previously mentioned. Because of the strategic location of many smaller cities, gangs have migrated because of the demand for drugs in those cities. One city in particular is Kenosha, Wisconsin, which is located halfway between Milwaukee and Chicago. Takata (1992) looked at gang activity in Kenosha, Wisconsin, which has a population of approximately eighty thousand.

The jobless rate in Kenosha was found to be at 9.8 percent, and 13 percent of Kenosha households were living below the poverty level (US Department of Labor, 1989). At the time of this study, African Americans and Hispanics comprised 7.6 percent of the city's population (US Bureau of Census, 1980). Like many other cities, Kenosha was caught off guard when the gangs first came. Police officers did not pay attention to the graffiti and gang symbols that were plastered on walls. Furthermore, they did not know what the gang symbols were.

As time passed, there was an increase in discipline problems that led officials to become more aware of gang problems. As the gang problems increased, so did the violence. In the Kenosha area, police observed a 25 percent increase in violations by juveniles (Wisconsin Office of Justice Assistance, 1985). In the Kenosha study, it was found that the gang problem originated mainly because of an influx of poor people from the slums of Chicago. In fact, one police officer gave Kenosha the name Cabrini North in reference to Cabrini Green, which was a poor and depressed area of Chicago. The other reason for the influx of the poor was that many saw Wisconsin and this area in particular as a welfare magnet. Many families simply wanted a better life.

Unfortunately, the dysfunctionality of the family unit does not disappear when the family moves from Chicago or elsewhere. If there are strong affiliations upon departure from a large metropolitan area, those affiliations will probably take root in a new location. In many instances, the roots may be stronger when drugs are involved because the gangs are positioning for dominance, control, and territorial rights. Moreover, the new location can be fertile ground for a lucrative drug trade for many gang members.

In terms of family dynamics, nothing has changed. In most cases, the single mother is struggling to survive and hoping to control her often out-of-control adolescent. In many other smaller cities, there is an influx of poor African Americans coming from large metropolitan areas and establishing gang ties. At the same time, the majority population is paranoid and suspicious of all African Americans moving into their cities and towns. The Kenosha study is a microcosm of what is occurring on a national level when it comes to gangs and how they are looked at by society at large. The innercity gang member is someone who is feared because of his propensity for criminal activities.

When the inner-city gang member is incarcerated, his gang affiliation does not cease; instead, his gang mentality and his rank follow him into the prison system. Prison officials usually know who is affiliated with what gang, but little can be done about it unless the youth flashes gang symbols or colors or engages in group resistance or other gang activities. Many of these gang members are also housed with rival gang members they knew on the streets before being incarcerated. Some have even been a boyfriend of another gang member's sister.

Because of the structured and punitive environment of the prison, almost always, rival gang members coexist without a great deal of difficulty. The prison environment is also a fertile breeding ground for recruitment. Gangs are pervasive in the Illinois Department of Corrections, and they are insidious, violent, organized and sophisticated (Lane, 1989).

Lane (1989) also estimates that 80 to 90 percent of the inmates in the Illinois correctional system have some affiliation with street gangs. The same percentage probably holds true in most prisons across the country.

When the inner-city gang member enters the prison system, he usually has an extensive criminal record. It is not unusual for many of these adolescents to have started getting in trouble with the police when they were nine or ten years old. Issues of abandonment, neglect, and abuse are also usually rampant. When the adolescent reaches the prison system, his behavior is usually intractable, and he is recalcitrant in attempting to change his negative behavior. Lane (1989) states that in many cases, entire families become gang members.

It is not uncommon for an inner-city incarcerated adolescent to report that his father is or was incarcerated and at one time belonged to a street gang. With the absence of the father and often the unconscious modeling of his behavior by the youth, one can see how and why the youth would be lured to gangs. Moreover, he has followed a generational trend whereby incarceration is seen as the norm, and this is what is expected of him. Additionally, jail or prison is a rite of passage for him, not only because his father has been incarcerated but also because most of his friends have been also. This institutionalization becomes a self-fulfilling prophecy. Furthermore, the adolescent has already made up in his mind that high school and, in particular, graduating from high school are not options for him.

Just as the community feels it is at war with gang members, prison officials feel the same way about inmates who are gang members. Lane (1989) states that the Illinois prison system considers itself at war with gang members. Gangs are pervasive throughout most prison systems throughout the United States. Lane (1989) also states that on September 3, 1987, unit superintendent Robert Taylor, a high-ranking official at the Pontiac Correctional Center, was stabbed and bludgeoned in his cellhouse office by two inmates who were later found to be gang chieftains. This type of ruthless behavior only highlights the fact that gang members will stop at nothing to control prisons, just as they attempt to control their neighborhoods.

It is also interesting to note that when many inner-city African American adolescents arrive at the reception center of a correctional facility, all of them are questioned about their prior drug usage. A high percentage of these adolescents has a history of polysubstance abuse. They also report a strong history of familial alcohol abuse as well as other substances. However, in many instances, marijuana is the drug of choice. It is also important to note that marijuana is much more potent than it was twenty years ago. With this potency comes more cognitive and emotional impairment in the younger user. Additionally, many adolescents in the correctional setting report that they smoke marijuana several times a day during any given week. A mixture of alcohol and marijuana can, in many cases, be quite deadly.

The correlation between alcohol use and aggressive behavior is well-documented. Alcohol consumption just prior to a violent crime is often reported (Collins, 1986). Also, gangster rap music is another crucial component that should be entered into the equation when examining adolescent homicides. The lyrics in many of these rap songs can be quite suggestive and evocative to the young listener. Many incarcerated adolescents have reported that they were listening to rap music prior to committing a serious crime. Many rap stars themselves believe in violence as a solution to conflict. This type of mindset, if you will, is passed down to young impressionable kids who idolize these rap stars.

Bushman and Cooper (1990) state that intoxication could impair an adolescent cognitively and emotionally. This may also be true when the adolescent listens to gangster rap music. In many instances, when listening to this type of music, there is a degree of emotional impairment because the adolescent has been programmed to act in a violent manner. Furthermore, when a record company that produces rap music is named Death Row Music Company, the name itself is suggestive of criminal behavior. It could be that the adolescent feels that anything goes.

Collins (1986) postulates that there are psychopharmacological effects of intoxication, which include disinhibition, cognitive perceptual distortions, attention deficits, etc. In conversing with many incarcerated inner-city adolescents, it is not uncommon to find that many of them report that they get less than an adequate amount of sleep. Pemanen (1981) discussed sleep deprivation and nutritional deficits as being contributing factors to aggressive behaviors. It is well-known that in the general adult population, when one is deprived of sleep, one can become very irritable and easy to anger. When the adolescent engages in polysubstance abuse, this can also affect the behavior of an already fragile and tenuous youth.

The Institute on Black Chemical Abuse (1990) states that 100,000 people die every year from alcohol-related causes. It also reported that 50 percent of all homicides are alcohol-related. This malady continues to devastate the African American community. Alcohol and other drugs rob young people of a promising future, shatter lives and communities, and also destroy families. According to the Institute on Black Chemical Abuse (1990), alcohol is the most abused drug in the country.

In the early 1980s, crack cocaine was almost unheard of in the African American community, but this deadly drug has since permeated every inner city in America (Inciardi, 1992). Although cocaine usage in general is more prevalent in the suburbs, the inner cities of America have been devastated by the crack cocaine epidemic (Staples, 1990). According to Wade Nobles, a social psychologist, the prevalence of drugs in the African American community, with its concomitant violence, has served to reduce the quantity and quality of African American life. He further stated that drug abuse has become an American condition. A former drug dealer confessed, "I didn't know that I was selling death to my people when I was peddling crack. We need you to teach us to love the African American culture because the drug culture has its arms wide open for young brothers" (White, 1990, p.18).

Staples (1990) posits that crack cocaine, because of its relatively cheap price, has had a tremendous negative impact on the African American community and the African American family. He further states that the peculiar nature of crack cocaine addiction has exacerbated the already existing problems of crime, poverty, unemployment, and racism. Staples (1990) further states that: (1) Children are taking over as heads of their families, largely because of their incomes from selling crack; (2) young, pregnant teens are risking their lives to secure the drug and in some cases exchanging sexual relations for it or the money to buy it; (3) some adolescents are deserting their families and forming violent gangs to sell and buy crack.

In many inner cities, there are turf wars between rival gangs for control of territories and the right to sell drugs in those areas. Many of the homicides that are committed by adolescents in the inner cities result from the drug war and gang disputes. Nobles (1980) postulates that the young inner-city African American male's involvement in drug activity impact on African American family life in many other ways. Nobles believes that the drug culture is creating a psychopathic environment where effective family functioning is not determined by the rules or moral values of one's social-cultural group but by the dictates of a system of deviancy and chaos.

Nobles also stated that those individuals and families who are involved in drug-taking and drug activity become consumed in that particular lifestyle. For them, this becomes primary in all social relationships. In some instances, adolescents will sell crack to their own parents. Many incarcerated adolescents have reported selling crack to their parents. This appears to be a role reversal whereby the adolescent is in a power position. This perceived power goes beyond the family and into the community where the adolescent will, on occasion, intimidate others in a violent fashion that will often lead to murder.

Spunt (et al.,1994) conducted an interview with 268 homicide offenders in New York State correctional facilities and found that 19 percent of homicides were reported to have been related to alcohol use. It was also found that many of these homicides resulted from arguments or disputes, and the respondents reported that they were high on at least one other substance.

At a 1980 symposium on "Homicide Among African American Males," this observation was made: More African Americans were killed in 1977 than died in the entire nine years of the Vietnam War (Alcohol, Drug Abuse, and Mental Health Administration, 1980:549). African Americans killed in combat in Vietnam between 1963 and 1972 numbered 5,640; but in 1977, a total of 5,734 African Americans were killed by other African Americans in the United States.

Busch (1990) postulates that adolescents who kill have a tetrad of symptoms: (1) criminally violent family members; (2) gang membership; (3) severe educational difficulties; and (4) alcohol abuse.

Crack cocaine is not listed probably because the impact of its devastation may not have been felt in the inner cities when this study was reported. Much more research needs to be done in this area.

SELF-HATRED

The self-hatred theory has been floating around for a long time now. Many social theorists take the position that many homicides occur between African American males because there is a tendency on the part of many African Americans to denigrate one another because of the negative messages that are sent by the larger society about them.

Allen (1980) proposed a concept of sub-intentioned homicide. The point that he tries to make is that in such homicides, the victim may play a role in bringing about his own death, consciously or unconsciously, by provoking the murder. It's possible that the innercity African American adolescent male may be in such pain emotionally because of his own negative self-concept that he wishes death on himself but at the hands of someone else.

One example would be when the adolescent says to one of his peers, "Go ahead and blow me away" or while he may be challenging and or pushing the situation to the brink of disaster. Allen's theory is similar to Shneidman's (1976) concept of inimicality as it relates to suicide. Shneidman's definition of inimicality is "those qualities within the individual that are unfriendly toward the self." He also believes that these negative feelings can be turned outward. When this happens, the risk of a homicide occurring heightens.

It is important to alleviate the socioeconomic ills that plague the inner cities, but it is also extremely important to address the negative psychological dynamics that come into play in the African American community that contribute to homicides. All of the aforementioned variables should be closely examined, and homicide prevention centers should be strategically located as an intervention technique.

It is with a great sense of urgency that inner-city children are taught early on how to deal with interpersonal conflict and to oppose violent confrontations. Moreover, if these children are taught early on not to devalue themselves, they will, at the same time, value the lives of others.

THE IMPACT OF RACISM, DISCRIMINATION, AND PREJUDICE

When inner-city African American males are incarcerated for various crimes, including homicides, it is easy for them to take a victim-stance position and feel that society has given them a raw deal because of their race. Many of these adolescents have no understanding of their history or how they've gotten to where they are in time. It is important to know where one came from if one is to know where one is going.

The African American has a long and complicated history in this country. It has oftentimes been a history marred by violence, discrimination, injustice, and racism. If one were to ask how the impact of racism could lead one to commit a homicide, it would not be an easy question to answer, but this is a very significant component that must be examined when looking at the inner-city African American male homicide rate.

Racism is a transgenerational component that has been like a cancer eating at the heart of America's inner city for decades. Racism has also been a ticking time bomb that seems to have incremental explosive capabilities as it relates to homicides. Over the generations, America has engaged in what could be called "benign neglect" when dealing with African Americans. Due to apathy, neglect, and the exclusionary policies that were directed toward African Americans by their own country, our inner cities are combat zones that are feared by many people who live on the periphery as well as those who live within these zones.

Kids are dying at an alarming rate, and because they're poor and African American, no one seems to care. If these homicides occurred in suburbia, a state of emergency would be put in place. Also, people are content as long as the murderers kill each other and don't invade their neighborhoods.

It is also important that we utilize a historical perspective when attempting to make some sense out of the senseless homicides that are occurring in our inner cities today.

African Americans were first brought to this country as slaves in 1619. There is one glaring distinction between African Americans and other nationalities as it relates to the way in which they came to this country. African Americans were brought here against their will, while other nationalities possessed their freedom before they arrived in America. More importantly, they also maintained their sense of freedom and dignity after arriving in America. They were not cursed because of the color of their skin.

Jordan (1969) extensively examined the attitudes held by whites toward African Americans from the 1500s to the years when this country was a young republic. In his research, he discovered that equality, liberty, and justice were not intended to be applied to African Americans. When African Americans first came to this country, they were brutalized and exploited psychologically and economically. There was a great deal of sweat and toil put into building this country by African Americans, but they were unable to reap the true fruits of their labor.

In the South, many were murdered for being disobedient and disrespectful toward slave-owners and those who were not slave-owners. It was expected that African Americans would be subservient and docile. They were also pulled away from their families and their motherland.

After reaching America, intact families were further separated because of the lucrativeness of slave trading.

African Americans were also made to have disdain for the color of their skin. Black skin was synonymous with something evil or sinister. Even today, many people refer to black magic or a black cloud as being something negative or evil. If someone is the black sheep of the family, that person is ostracized or rejected. On the other hand, we frequently hear people say things like it is as pure as snow, which denotes that if the snow is white, it has to be pure. Even when people were found to have one speck of "black blood," they were considered to be black by law. Because of this, many people who actually did have one drop of black blood actually passed for white because of the preferential treatment they would receive by being a white person. This was also seen in the South when slave-owners would give preferential treatment to light-skinned African Americans by allowing them to perform domestic work while dark-skinned slaves worked in the fields.

In 1863, Abraham Lincoln legally freed the slaves from bondage. Even though they were free in the legal sense of the word, they were not truly free. Even after Reconstruction in the South, there were many barriers put in place that were oppressive in nature. A very serious and far-reaching mistake was made during this period. The mistake was that African Americans were not given full and equal status as American citizens. Segregated schools were put in place that were unequal academically. Many of the public accommodations used by African Americans were kept separate, and they were inferior to those used by whites.

African Americans were also not allowed to vote. If they attempted to vote, they were terrorized and, in many instances, lynched. If African Americans did not stay in their place, they were oftentimes severely punished by local governmental agencies. Even the federal government stood idly by as African Americans were brutalized, oppressed, and treated in an inhumane manner at the hands of white America. While all of this was occurring, there was very little insight into the chronicity of the psychological scarring that would eventually rip this nation apart for decades to come.

Because racism has been so ingrained in America, even psychologists and psychiatrists have been affected by racist practices, and this, in turn, affected their view of African Americans. All too often, these views have been negative in nature. Psychologists and psychiatrists should have taken a position against racism decades ago; instead, many of these clinicians went along with the status quo and treated African Americans as if they were subhuman. The racism that was perpetuated by a profession that was supposed to be humane, empathetic, and compassionate contributed to the present-day combat zones that are commonplace in most central cities across America. Each generation of African Americans has been severely affected by a society that viewed them as outcasts and degenerates.

These negative feelings have unfortunately been passed down from generation to generation. If one were to do an investigative study to examine the heritage of African Americans living in large American cities, one would find that a large majority of these individuals have roots in the American South. This is very crucial because the South was the seat of racism, prejudice, and discrimination. Even physicians in the South felt that African Americans could be treated only by white southern doctors. It was also argued by some that African Americans had a blunted sensibility of the nervous system. It was also asserted that the brain of the African American was much smaller than the brain of the white person.

Segregation of schools and other institutions throughout society was condoned because many psychologists and psychiatrists took the position that the African American was incapable of managing a high degree of civilization (Poussaint, 1984). Poussaint further states that many early psychiatrists took the position that the African American's psychological development was more childlike and less complex than that of his white counterpart.

Franklin (1989) posits that slavery set the tone for African Americans to be treated as inferior. Skin color was and is still today a badge of difference. Due to this difference, many inner cities are exclusively African American because whites have migrated to the suburbs. Moreover, businesses have left, and this has further crippled an already fragile economy. Blau and Blau (1982) posit that the expression of frustration in the form of violent crime is particularly pronounced when economic inequality is based upon ascriptive characteristics like race. The effects of economic inequality on African American homicide rates will be discussed further.

Racist-based humiliation directed against the African American community can also give one the impression that the police department is at war against the African American community, particularly the male African American community. In Boston, it was common practice for police officers to stop young African American males as they were leaving school and other places (Black Male Youth, 1990). It is this type of racial oppression that makes one cognizant of the fact that they're different in many ways, and society at large sees them as being violent and dangerous. Those on the periphery see inner cities as combat zones, and the residents of these areas see themselves as being under a state of siege by the police department.

It may also be difficult for one to see just how racism can impact the male adolescent homicide rate. To fully understand this concept, one must also understand the racist history of America. The African American male adolescent who lives in the inner city is a product of a society that told his parents, his grandparents, and his great-grandparents that they were unworthy of being full citizens and their skin color was a badge of difference. One might argue this point by saying that the Irish, Germans, and Italians came to this country, pulled themselves up by their bootstraps, and were accepted as full citizens; therefore, one might wonder why African Americans were not able to do likewise. One example of why this did not happen is that skin color was the main factor that prevented it from happening.

Germans and others who had white skin never had to worry about going to the back of the bus or having to drink from a "Germans only" water fountain as African Americans did. Moreover, while immigrants did not have to worry about going to segregated schools or not being able to educate their kids in a public school of their choice, African Americans had to. Also, if someone with Negroid features had come to this country from any African country and asked to be served in any restaurant in the South three or four decades ago, they more than likely would have been arrested. It didn't matter if this person was a minister, an engineer, a psychologist, or a world-renowned scientist or physician.

Many African Americans fled these discriminatory practices by migrating to cities in the east, north, and west. Many of them assumed they had found the American dream through employment, housing, and opportunities that were not available to them in the South. Many of them hit brick walls, if you will, and ended up living in dilapidated buildings in inner-city slums. In virtually every central city throughout America, poverty, blight, deterioration, and crime are repeated themes. Again, African Americans were forced to live in certain areas of the city.

Discrimination and segregation in housing patterns were all too prevalent across America. Invisible boundaries were put in place, and local officials worked extremely hard at making sure that African Americans stayed within a certain area of the city. Many white city dwellers were concerned about the areas in which they lived becoming ghettoized. For many decades, lending institutions and insurance companies engaged in redlining, whereby loans were not granted to African Americans in certain neighborhoods. Likewise, insurance companies refused to underwrite policies in certain areas. African Americans were further isolated and alienated because whites moved to the suburbs in large numbers to avoid what many saw as the takeover by an underclass. Many wanted their properties to appreciate rather than depreciate, and many felt that having African Americans as neighbors would cause their property to depreciate. This form of racism has been a fact of American life and is still deeply ingrained in the American psyche today.

Griffin (1991) talks about the rage that still exists in the African American community today. This rage has also been passed down to the adolescents. One way that this rage is exhibited is through homicidal behavior that is directed toward someone of the same color. Poussaint (1984) posited that racism can cause psychological scarring that can cause an individual to become a victimizer. African American adolescents, on an unconscious level, have taken on oppressive symptoms from the older generations. It's possible that these oppressive symptoms can cause the adolescent to feel that his own life has no meaning, and he in turn does not value the life of someone who looks like himself.

In essence, the adolescent may identify with the oppressor. The perpetrator of a homicide may also see the same features in his victim as he sees in himself. He may be extremely angry at the majority of society for its oppressive tendencies, and he may therefore, in turn, displace his anger and rage onto a mirror image of himself, which often is another African American male. The adolescent may also repress the hostile feelings that he has toward a society that he sees as unjust. On the other hand, it is also possible that he may express his hostile feelings toward another adolescent by committing a homicide. It's possible that he identifies with the oppressor because he sees his victim as having all of the characteristics that society has deemed unacceptable.

Throughout history, the African American has seen himself as the underdog (Griffin, 1991). Many African American males who live in the inner city expect to go to jail or prison. All too often, the news media highlights the fact that an African American male is being led off to jail in handcuffs.

Jenkins (1982) posits that minority groups that are negatively stereotyped and exploited by the larger society can learn to hate themselves and become self-destructive. Griffin (1991) believes that this dynamic can be observed among many adolescent African American males who have heard from the larger society that they are worthless, have been treated as worthless, and as a result, come to feel hopeless about themselves and their future. The sad fact is that many African American males are destroying both themselves and others with drugs, alcohol, and violent encounters with one another and the police. Many incarcerated African American adolescent males have commented, "I killed the 'Nigga' before he killed me." This is a prime example of the self-hatred directed toward a member of one's own group.

Grier and Cobbs (1968) stated that "African Americans continue to revolt against laws and customs that are deadly and humiliating." They further stated that "aggression leaps from wounds inflicted and ambitions spiked. It grows out of oppression and capricious cruelty." When Grier and Cobbs wrote these words, the African American communities across the country were revolting and rioting against racism. Today, the African American community has not yet reached that level of illustration; instead, the anger and rage that fueled riots have been turned inward to the self and onto others who look like the self.

Many inner-city African American adolescent males are extremely angry today. Much of this anger is directed toward the reflected self, the other African American male adolescent. Respect for the adolescent is not granted by the larger society; therefore, he gets his respect by taking someone else's life and looking like a big man in the eyes of his peers. He further feels that education will not make a difference in his life because he will not be accepted anyway.

W. E. B. DuBois (1904) states that "The Negro is a sort of seventh son, born with a veil, and gifted with second sight in this American world—a world which yields him no true self-consciousness, but only lets him see himself through the revelation of the other world. It is a peculiar sensation, this double consciousness, this sense of always looking at one's self through the eyes of others, of measuring one's soul by the tape of a world that looks on in amused contempt and pity."

As we enter the twenty-first century, inner-city as well as other African American males are still confronted and challenged by the "double consciousness" that W. E. B. DuBois spoke of in the first decade of the last century. Many of these young men may feel invisible, and doing something outrageous is certain to bring attention to them. Being an African American male—and more importantly, an inner-city African American male—one is confronted on a daily basis with the anxieties that come with being African American in a country that would prefer them to remain invisible.

Unfortunately, many inner-city African American males will tell you that they will do what they have to, to survive in a hostile world. This also means putting their lives on the line or taking someone else's life on the battlefield that they call home. In any society, when people feel valued and needed, they will reciprocate by being productive. On the other hand, if it is self-evident that a society has no desire for your presence or any need for you as a person, this in turn can produce tension, strain, anger, and rage.

After the age of twelve, the inner-city adolescent has had ample time to explore his world and make a determination as to how he fits into the scheme of things. His worldview is often a negative one, and many of these adolescents do not see themselves living past the age of twenty-one. Their worldview has been largely shaped by the larger society because they are constantly bombarded with images that depict them as being a member of the permanent underclass. Many of them feel that no one cares about them, so they have the attitude that they're going to get what they deserve by being hedonistic and narcissistic without regard for others.

The present generation of poor inner-city African American males is unique in terms of their skewed worldview. They are the offspring of a generation that had a false sense of economic security. Also, the previous generation was very hedonistic, and in the midst of the turmoil, the kids were lost. The decrease in values and morality caused a wider schism between the previous generation and the present generation.

In many American cities, racial segregation is a fact of life. Fifteen to twenty years ago, it was thought that progress was being made in this area. Again, there was a false sense of security in terms of social and economic gains made by African Americans. The white power bases moving out of many inner cities further eroded the economic stability of many inner-city African American families.

Balkwell (1990) posits that the social and economic inequality that African Americans experience increases criminogenic consequences. Even though many adolescents may not be quite ready to join the workforce, their feelings of anger and frustration may derive from the fact that their parents or parent may be struggling to make ends meet. These economic hardships that most inner-city African American families must confront on a daily basis can produce a tremendous amount of stress and tension. When people are under a tremendous amount of stress, it is easy to become angry and volatile.

Blau and Blau (1982) contend that frustration in the form of violent crime is particularly pronounced when economic inequality is based on race.

Denton and Massey (1988) posit that segregation in housing between African Americans and whites is a pervasive aspect of racial inequality in the United States. They further stated that prejudice and discrimination in the housing market produce residential environments that are separated largely along racial lines.

Hogan and Kitagawa (1985) found that these segregated communities provide a markedly different social environment for their residents. High rates of unemployment, welfare dependency, dilapidated housing, high infant mortality, unwed motherhood, and crime pervade African American neighborhoods. Similarly, poorer schools and high taxes plague African American neighborhoods (Massey, 1990).

Blau and Blau (1982) outlined some of the mechanisms by which racial residential segregation could have a critical influence on homicides: "Racial segregation imposes a significant barrier to African American upward mobility and quality of life. Place of residence locates people not only in geographic space but also in networks of social opportunities—it influences prospects for employment, for public services, for educational advancement, for appreciation in home values, and more. Residential segregation by race accordingly, implies that opportunities for achievement are limited for certain groups, and in conflict with basic American value commitments that encourage members of all groups to strive for socioeconomic success. Such a 'disjuncture' between structural arrangements and fundamental cultural values tends to undermine the legitimacy of social norms and thereby promotes deviant behavior."

Inner-city African American males today seem to be much more affected by the mechanisms outlined by Blau and Blau. As one drives through any inner city of America today, one can plainly see that the dilapidation, the anger, and the level of social distress have heightened to an alarming level.

Sampson (1985) found that higher residential segregation is associated with higher levels of murder. Massey (1990) stated that one important consequence of the "American apartheid of residence is an increased level of lethal violence for African Americans." This in turn causes a tremendous amount of strain, tension, frustration, and aggression that is displaced onto others whose plights are similar to those of the perpetrator, in most cases. Economic conditions in the inner cities have reached an all-time low, and it appears that these conditions will get worse before they get better.

The inner-city African American adolescent male, in most cases, can experience a tremendous amount of anxiety centering around his plight and the inequities that he sees in society. He may engage in denial whenever negative thoughts and feelings cause him to experience anxiety. The anxiety may cause him to become frustrated, and the frustration, in turn, may cause him to become aggressive. It is highly probable that self-hatred, anger, and rage are fueling his displaced aggression when he takes the life of another African American adolescent male.

CHAPTER 3

DISCUSSION AND RECOMMENDATIONS

It is important for teachers, clinicians, and others who come in contact with poor inner-city African American male adolescents on a daily basis to be able to recognize flamboyance, swaggering, and extreme acting out as possible signs of depression. Often, people are too quick to enforce punitive measures rather than examine the underlying causes of the behavior. It is extremely important for those involved with this population to consider the ramifications of masked depression or agitated depression.

When the majority of society observes many poor inner-city African American male adolescents engaging in self-effacing behavior, they are quick to write them off as thugs, failures, criminals, drug dealers, and scum.

Many people are quick to sponsor poverty-stricken children from Third World countries but are unwilling to come to the aid of inner-city adolescent males who, if nurtured, could probably contribute much to society. If these children know that they are cared about, there would be no need to mask their feelings or to take a posturing stance. Moreover, there would be no need for them to take another's life because their own lives would be full of hope and meaning.

Adolescents usually respond in a positive way to love and discipline. Replacing absent fathers with mentors would decrease the level of frustration, isolation, and alienation found in many of these adolescents. When biological fathers don't claim paternity, this may cause the adolescent to become more resentful and vengeful. There is also a tendency on the part of women to withdraw and pull away from the father of their child through separation or divorce. For the mental stability of the child and adolescent, it is important for the father and the mother to work in a cooperative and collaborative fashion for the benefit of the child. It is well-known that when loss or abandonment occurs, depression can follow.

Financial support from the fathers of abandoned adolescents is not enough. Emotional support through the formative years is crucial for the development of a psychologically balanced adolescent and adult. If the adolescent feels that someone cares about him, he will, in turn, care about others. It is important to try to change the childhood schemas that can lead to depression. If the parent has negative schemas, the child may emulate these same schemas; therefore, working with these at-risk families from early on is extremely crucial. When the family is strengthened, the individual is strengthened. Public schools can also be very instrumental in implementing programs that involve the family.

There is also a tremendous amount of learned helplessness on the part of these adolescents. Because of the deadness and the hopelessness, many of these adolescents give up. For many of them, their lives are filled with disappointments and many negative events. It's possible that the depression and hopelessness that they feel can manifest itself in the form of extreme acting out behavior. If masked depression can be treated through psychotherapeutic intervention, the likelihood of an adolescent's committing a homicide can be greatly decreased. Early childhood intervention should take precedence over incarceration.

For some, depression may seem an insignificant variable, but it may be a crucial component to the puzzle of adolescent homicides. Future research should be done in this area to shed light on this very critical topic.

As long as inner-city residents continue to allow drugs, gangs, and alcohol to flourish, the homicides will continue to occur. The sad fact is that many citizens turn their backs on the day-to-day violence that devastates their communities. Police officers cannot do it all. If things are to change, residents have to respect one another and, if necessary, police their own communities. Many people do not take a stand when garbage is strewn throughout their neighborhoods. Liquor stores are plentiful, and drug deals in broad daylight are common occurrences. Unless there is an uprising of the general citizenry, nothing will change. Law-abiding citizens who live in the inner city are often too tolerant of the sinister activities that produce the blight and the high murder rates. When families decide to rise up and not be held hostage by gangs or otherwise, then things will change.

It also appears that the war on drugs is not working. This is a multibillion-dollar-a-year industry, and in order for the flow of drugs to be stopped from coming into inner cities, it has to be stopped not when it reaches the inner cities but when it's in the hands of drug lords who do not live in the inner city.

Many poor inner-city adolescents are vulnerable to drug trafficking and other deviant response patterns because of neglect, abandonment, modeling, negative feedback, and negative self-attitudes. In order to change these dynamics, one must focus on intervention strategies early on. The schools, the churches, and the entire community must get involved. The negative self-images have to be changed at a very early age. This is a tremendous task that lies ahead. If this society is to be unified, these problems have to be solved.

Since stress in the poor inner-city African American adolescent male can be insidious, early childhood intervention is extremely important. All too often, this population is very poor at handling interpersonal conflict. Conflict resolution should be introduced in the schools as early as kindergarten and continued through all grades. If this occurs, then the negative childhood schemas that often result in an adolescent's committing a homicide could be altered at a very early age.

If a child can learn to reason at an early age, he can also be taught positive coping skills; therefore, stress inoculation techniques should be taught in the early grades so that the child will be able to recognize triggers later on in life that indicate that he's dealing with an emotional overload. Moreover, he will have the skills to navigate his way through difficult situations. Individuals in anger-management groups have often talked about how being in the group helped them navigate their way through volatile situations. This should be an integral part of the school's curriculum starting early on.

Many of these adolescents are extremely vulnerable to the negative things in their environment. They are also presented with a double-edged sword in that often the parents or parent cannot cope effectively. Because of the negativism held by the parents and their inability to cope, it is crucial that these families are identified and in-home counseling is instituted so as to bring a sense of balance to the family. Some of these families will use alcohol to dampen their emotional pain, but in many instances, they are unaware of the real reasons that they choose to abuse alcohol.

Often, when families are poor, it helps to provide an incentive when trying to engage them in various programs that would be beneficial to the family. Monetary or other incentives would propel families to participate in seminars, explaining the dangers of alcohol and how it impacts negatively on the family. When individuals are involved in automobile accidents frequently, they are required to participate in a defensive driving course. Likewise, when alcohol or drugs are abused in the family, or family members are abused by parents or a parent, courses in parenting should be mandated by law. If the family cannot be a buffer in times of chaos and confusion, who can the adolescent turn to? In times of stress, usually the gang is his first choice. If the family can maintain its strength and cohesiveness, the adolescent might not be lured to the gang.

Society has a big responsibility of embracing the inner-city African American male and making him feel as if he is an integral part of our nation. This should be done by providing positive images instead of the negative ones that are often flashed across newspapers and television screens. If the adolescent does not feel rejected, this will exponentially decrease his frustration and thereby decrease his level of aggression.

It is also important to impress upon absent African American fathers how crucial it is for them to become actively involved in the lives of their sons at an early age. If the child feels loved instead of abandoned, his stress tolerance will greatly increase. The psychological distress of being abandoned may also contribute to the development of an antisocial personality.

By the time the inner-city African American male reaches adolescence, a great deal of psychic numbing has taken place because of the many stressors he has had to face. When American servicemen returned home from Vietnam, many of them suffered from post-traumatic stress disorder due to the many casualties and fatalities that they witnessed while in combat. The poor inner-city African American male has also witnessed violence and homicides, but no post-traumatic stress intervention has taken place. When death occurs in a suburban school setting, grief counselors are called in immediately. In the inner city, death is seen as an everyday occurrence, and no type of therapeutic intervention is put in place. Doing nothing means that no one cares, and this has to change if society expects to see a shift in the inner-city African American male homicide rate.

There is no clear-cut evidence, but it is also possible that a fetus is affected by stress in utero. Again, education is paramount in helping women to understand the multitude of dangers that can befall them during the gestation period.

Finally, the church has always been a fortress in the African American community. Today, more than ever before, inner-city churches of all denominations should unite and establish as their primary agenda a strategy to reunite the family and provide strong leadership and mentoring for the African American adolescent male. In today's society, handguns are quite prevalent. It is also extremely easy for anyone in society to purchase a handgun. Sheley (1993) looked at gun-possession among juvenile adolescents. He found that owning and carrying guns are fairly common behaviors among segments of the juvenile population. When inner-city African American adolescents are questioned as to why they carry guns, many of them will tell you that they are "strapped" because everyone else is carrying a gun and that they will not be caught with their guard down. This mindset has to be challenged. If no one takes a strong position on this issue, the perpetrators of homicides will more than likely become younger and younger, which could also mean that their level of impulse control is much lower.

It is going to be a tremendous task to disarm the thousands of youth that carry handguns. Those individuals who sell these handguns to inner-city youth need to have a consciousness-raising experience; it appears that the retailers are numb to the devastation caused by these firearms. As long as inner-city adolescents are killing each other, it doesn't matter as long as there is a profit made from the gun trade. Stricter penalties should also be enforced for carrying a weapon.

In the schools, we teach our kids at a very early age not to approach strangers. It is also just as important to teach them at a very early age the devastating effects of guns. Inner-city residents should not sit back and wait for our government to institute policies on gun control; instead, there should be a concerted effort to teach morals and values at a very early age. In many instances, the African American adult population is afraid to approach or interact with inner-city African American adolescents because they fear for their own safety. This phenomenon also appears to be getting worse instead of better. If this indifference and alienation continues, increased chaos and destruction will also continue.

In many cities, police departments have instituted gun buyback programs where residents can turn in their guns and be paid for them with no questions asked. Even if an individual turns in a gun, he can access another one just as easily as he did before. Also, he may have had more than one gun in his possession initially. Therefore, in terms of preventing homicides, it doesn't help. If the United States told the former Soviet Union that instead of aiming one thousand nuclear warheads at them, they were going to reduce the number to one hundred nuclear warheads, what sense would it make if only one hundred nuclear weapons could destroy the country one hundred times over? Any way you look at it, total destruction would occur.

In the case of the inner-city adolescent African American male, it may be more important to attempt to alter his belief system as a first priority. Many inner-city adolescents do not believe that they can survive in their neighborhoods without being armed. If things are to change, the entire community must stand up and be cohesive in their commitment to restore peace and order in their respective communities.

It also appears that there has been a gradual disintegration of the family over the last two decades. This chaos has brought a tremendous amount of confusion to the already shattered lives of innercity adolescents. Many states are already starting to dismantle welfare programs, but many families are vulnerable because the aftershocks are going to devastate many families. To date, very few safety nets are being put in place to protect the children. Because of the many years of learned helplessness, day-to-day survival will be a struggle for many families.

In order to reduce the violence and destruction of lives, not only inner-city African Americans but all African Americans must return to being their brother's keepers if any semblance of sanity is to be restored. The government can't do this alone. Each individual plays a vital part in restoring order in their own community. It serves no purpose to wear a

T-shirt that says "Respect one another" when the action is not carried through. There must also be a strengthening of moral consciousness as well as a sense of identity.

Poor inner-city residents are the least likely to seek psychological help because of the stigma attached to seeing a psychologist. If the high homicide rate is to be halted, at-risk families have to be identified and in home psychotherapeutic services must be rendered to help these families cope and be able to deal with the anger, rage, helplessness, and hopelessness that many of them feel. For any society, if there is a weak link in the chain, the society is only as strong as its weakest link.

It is unfortunate that racism permeates all of society. In sum, homicides among African American male adolescents are a systematic expression of what racism does to human beings in a nation where the reality is "us" and "them." If the racist determinants were reduced, one would surmise that homicides could also be reduced. When one looks at the history of South Africa, it is quite evident that apartheid subjugated and alienated black Africans in that country. South Africa is now seeing the devastating effects of its past racial policies in the township of Soweto and in the city of Johannesburg, South Africa. Black South Africans are now killing each other at an alarming rate because of anger, rage, and self-hatred.

There is a parallel between what is going on in that country and in the United States as it relates to the homicide rate among blacks. The playing field must be level, and equal opportunity must be extended to all citizens in order for each one to have a healthy self-concept. When America prizes the contributions and talents of all of its citizens, a downturn in homicides among African American males will occur.

It is a known fact that if a dog suspects he is feared, he will retreat with his tail between his legs or he will attack. The inner-city African American male is feared by the larger society, and he can therefore react in an aggressive manner or take on negative characteristics that allow him to feel potent or masculine on his own terms. Many people see his actions as that of a subculture, and the prefix *sub* can denote a deficiency that is inherent. Such terms as *sub* and *disadvantaged* may leave the adolescent with the notion that something about him is flawed, and he may in turn act out these expectancies. It is therefore crucial for policy-makers and others to take an honest look at their own prejudices and biases when attaching labels and implementing policies that adversely affect these youth.

We do live in a country that prides itself on its natural resources. For example, if the population of the bald eagle appears to be becoming extinct, millions of dollars are channeled into finding ways to protect this population from extinction.

Homicides among African American males should also be given top priority in expending prevention funds. The African Americans came to this country as a proud people, and the African American male should be viewed as a valuable asset that can only strength our position in the world. It is paramount that money be directed toward research that can uncover the root causes of homicides among this population.

African American males have fought and died valiantly in every war that has been fought by America. They have also made many contributions in many fields. It is apparent that African Americans have always wanted to be a part of this country, and research is badly needed to determine why so many choose to drop out as well as destroy the lives of those who look like themselves.

The Alcohol, Drug Abuse, and Mental Health Administration (1980) compiled data on homicides. They found that 54 percent of all homicides were committed by persons under the age of eighteen. This statistic may be even higher now because the family base has been eroded, violent gangs are more prevalent, and the crack cocaine epidemic has expanded. The data from their study also indicate that lack of academic achievement and high truancy rates are strongly associated with delinquency. Many personality and behavioral patterns that are associated with delinquent youth have also been identified. When many adolescents enter the correctional setting, they tend to exhibit a great deal of anger, conduct disorders, depressive symptoms, and antisocial patterns of behavior.

Another salient feature is that they have had multiple suspensions or expulsions from school. This should be a red flag because it's an indication that severe trouble lies ahead for them. The multiple suspensions and expulsions are often indicative of severe family problems that the child or adolescent finds extremely difficult to deal with in an effective manner. He therefore takes on maladaptive patterns of behavior to cope with the negative events in his life. Aside from the parent or parents, teachers and school administrators have the most contact with the child or adolescent. School officials should be highly trained in assessing the child's level of functioning and deviant patterns of behavior. When these deviant patterns are recognized, a multidisciplinary approach should be implemented, whereby the child is mentored and counseled on a constant and consistent basis. If one waits until the child or adolescent gets into trouble repetitively, it may be too late to save him. Since many inner-city African American males tend to shut down educationally at an early age, it's crucial to examine the reasons why. When the child or adolescent is expelled from school, in-home tutoring should be provided as well as mentoring so that the individual does not lag behind educationally. His expulsion or suspension may be a cry for help because he knows no other way to cope. If he knows that others truly care about him, he will more than likely cooperate with school officials. There also has to be collaboration between the school and the parent. Furthermore, if he knows that his world is safe, his academic performance will increase. In order to see a drop in the homicide rate of inner-city African American males, it is crucial that schools take the lead in turning around the lives of these troubled youth.

Churches and community organizations must also put these males under a protective umbrella when the family can't do it. Religion has always been a vital part of the African American community, and it must continue to play a vital role in the community. Many younger African Americans have pulled away from religion, something that has sustained this population for centuries. If many of these families can reestablish their religious ties, they may be able to bring a sense of balance to their lives as well as a sense of purpose. Often, adolescents in general will deviate from the morals and values of their parents, but if those values are instilled early on, they will, in time, come full circle with the beliefs that they learned in childhood. This is to say that even though they may stray in adolescence, the teaching from their childhood is carried into adulthood.

Because a significant number of families will lose a son to violence, it is important that clinicians know how to deal with the bereaved parents and other relatives so as to assist them in putting their shattered lives back together. Moreover, the problem of the African American male homicide rate needs immediate attention if we are to turn these shattered lives around. In many instances, the victim as well as the perpetrator have a great deal to offer society when time and energy are spent with them in a mentoring fashion. Rather than blaming the perpetrator for his "psychopathology," psychologists should lead the way in eradicating all of the variables that lead adolescents down a road of death and destruction.

What is needed now is early childhood intervention programs where not just the kids are involved but also the parents. If there is a total and full understanding of why these homicides occur, then there is a good chance that by intervening early on, we can drastically decrease these staggering statistics and bring a sense of balance and unity to families at the same time. If a community is stable and healthy, then its inhabitants will be balanced, secure, safe, and concerned about the individual welfare of one another. In many depressed communities, this does not occur. In examining some of the contributing psychological variables that may cause African American adolescent homicides, it is hoped that this critical analysis will guide us in the direction of alleviating this problem as we enter the twenty-first century.

Every adult has a responsibility to do his or her share in bringing an end to these tragic deaths because these children are our most valuable resources.

Erickson (1963) stated that "there is in every child at every stage, a new miracle of vigorous unfolding, which constitutes a new hope and new responsibility for all." Many of these children never received a chance to bloom or unfold.

In closing, it is appropriate to quote Aimee Cesaire (1972) who stated that "A [nation] that proves incapable of solving the problems it creates, is a decadent [nation]. A [nation] that chooses to close its eyes to its most crucial problems is a stricken [nation]. A [nation] that uses its principles for trickery and deceit is a dying [nation]."

CLINICAL IMPLICATIONS

It is extremely critical that professional schools of psychology and other graduate schools in psychology not only prepare future psychologists for dealing with the inner-city African American male but also thoroughly train mental health specialists in the African American experience.

Many clinicians will refuse to see an African American adolescent male who is perceived as being racist and hostile. Clinicians who deal with this population must be aware of where the client is coming from and where the client is in the here and now. This population of clients is very good at detecting whether the therapist really cares about their welfare. Therapists, at the same time, must examine their own consciousness for their own personal biases.

The inner-city African American male adolescent has experienced rejection most of his life, and the therapist must be careful not to come across in a condescending way. Often it takes a tremendous amount of work and patience to establish rapport with this group of adolescents. Many will seem incorrigible, but the therapist has to remember that behind the defensive shield is a person who is hurting emotionally but does not know how to reach out for help. Usually he has experienced a great deal of emotional trauma and often physical trauma. Moreover, therapists must be cognizant of the extreme possibility of neglect, deprivation, and family drug abuse. The therapist needs to let this client know that in his world of deadness, despair, and helplessness, there is still hope. Many of these adolescents do not believe that graduating from high school is an attainable goal. Even more distressing, many do not see themselves living past the age of twenty-one.

The therapist must also keep in mind that there is a broad spectrum of abilities within this population. Many psychologists like to use the term *low-functioning*. A person may be low-functioning but may also be the best mechanic in town. Also, a person with an IQ of 80 may be extremely good at many different things. It is important for the therapist to accent the positives and not take the position that low-functioning means that the adolescent has no place in society. The therapist must also be aware that these adolescents lag in many areas because of truancy, family dynamics or dysfunctionality, and other stressors in the environment.

Acting out behavior may also be a sign of depression in the adolescent. He may engage in swaggering and posturing to deal with his intense anger and frustration. At the same time, the therapist must be careful not to over-pathologize. One needs to be aware that therapeutic intervention would be efficacious over a correctional facility in many cases.

In talking with many of these adolescents, it has been reported that they feel a great deal of "deadness" and boredom in their lives. Often these adolescents will create excitement by engaging in criminal activity. The therapist needs to be aware that much of this severe acting out behavior is generated by helplessness, hopelessness, anger, frustration, and despair.

Many of these adolescents have not seen or had contact with their fathers. This can cause a great deal of anger that manifests itself in many different forms. The therapist has to be aware of transference issues. Often the adolescent will see the male therapist as a father figure, and the therapist must decide how he wants to handle this. Many adolescents will not want to talk about the absent father but yet harbor a great deal of anger and rage toward him. This is something that the therapist can help the adolescent to deal with. Usually when the anger and the rage dissipate, the adolescent is able to engage in cognitive restructuring.

The adolescent also tends to idolize his mother, whether she's right or wrong. The mother-son dyad is generally strong, and the therapist must be aware of this relationship. The adolescent usually protects the mother and can be extremely sensitive to negative comments made about the mother.

The adolescent also has the perception that seeing a psychologist means that one is "crazy." This is a cultural dictate that the therapist should be aware of. The adolescent is afraid of what people will say about him if it's disseminated that he is seeing a psychologist. The therapist can allay these fears and concerns by fully explaining to the adolescent the role of a psychologist and reassuring him as to his level of mental competency.

Finally, the therapist must be aware that racism does exist and he/she needs to be aware of how it impacts the life of the adolescent. If the therapist is Caucasian, he or she may want to find out how the adolescent feels about Caucasians. Having an African American therapist does not mean that the therapist is exempt. An African American therapist has to be careful that he or she does not belittle or look down on the client. This can easily happen because the therapist may not be comfortable with himself as an African American and may see the client as an epitome of the problem. It is therefore important for the therapist to examine his consciousness and to feel good about who he or she is. The client should be treated with empathy, dignity, and respect.

IMPLICATIONS FOR FUTURE RESEARCH

Homicides committed by inner-city African American adolescent males against other inner-city African American males is a problem that is growing at an alarming rate. Many young adolescents are being waived to adult correctional facilities, and adolescent facilities are gearing up to accept kids as young as ten years of age. Many states have allocated funds for the purpose of building what is called the "supermax" prison. These maximum-security prisons will house the most dangerous and incorrigible inmates.

Unfortunately, for many of these African American adolescent males, there will be no second chance. Thousands of these adolescents will never experience the joys of raising families or experience the liberties and freedoms that can be easily taken for granted. It is almost incomprehensible, but these juvenile offenders will spend all of their teen years as well as their adult life behind prison bars. The nation's "get tough policy" on criminals will make it impossible for many of them ever to be paroled.

Much research has been done in the past to uncover why these murders are occurring. Even though the research continues to flow, the murders continue, and the prisons continue to be constructed.

Theories relating to aggression have addressed this problem, but the implementations of intervention strategies have not been put in place. The funds that are allocated for prisons should be utilized for research purposes when the child is in the infant stage or even in utero. Most of the emphasis is directed toward the adolescent who commits a homicide, but the mother-son dyad as well as the fatherson dyad should be studied extensively.

Research shows that aggression starts early on and that it's a learned process. This being true, it can also be unlearned. The schools can do a great deal in teaching the child how to be nonaggressive, but the family is even more crucial in solving this problem.

One cannot dictate morals and values nor can one tell others what their parenting style should be; however, many inner-city African American mothers are under a tremendous amount of stress due to financial hardships and the task of raising children in a hostile environment.

Future research should look at educational enhancement programs that will help these mothers to feel good about themselves and to help them to become marketable as far as finding stable employment. Moreover, the emotional burdens must be taken off the mothers.

In order to raise a family adequately, one needs to be able to supply them with adequate medical, dental, and life insurance and other necessities without feeling burdened from paycheck to paycheck. In order for this to happen, industry must come back to the inner cities, and job training must take place on a massive scale. Future research may best be focused on ways to strengthen the family. Even though many of these families are female-headed, this unit has to remain stable if stability is to be expected in adolescence. It is also important not to forget the fathers. Even though many of them are absent, attention should be focused on getting them involved with their children. Research should also be focused on why they chose to distance themselves from their children.

Drugs play a major part in homicides, and there has to be a massive sweep in eradicating drugs from inner-city neighborhoods. This is a multibillion-dollar-a-year industry, and there has to be more than lip service when it comes to eradicating this deadly menace. Often, African Americans end up in correctional facilities when, in fact, a drug treatment center would have better served them.

Crack cocaine has left a tremendous amount of destruction in its path, and it is crucial that this deadly scourge be brought to a halt. Future research should focus on why individuals choose to destroy their minds and bodies. The long-term effects of cocaine usage are not completely known. This is also an area that should lend itself to future research.

This study examines psychocultural variables that contribute to homicides. Although these variables are theoretical in nature, they can be further examined, and many other variables can also be added to the existing list. It may be impossible to predict who will commit a homicide, but given the information provided, intervention strategies can be implemented early on that can prevent many of these homicides from occurring.

Lastly, racism continues to cause a tremendous amount of frustration, anger, and helplessness among many inner-city African Americans. Much has been written about racism, but future research needs to continue to deal with this topic and its impact on the homicide rate in the African American community.

RESEARCH REFERENCES

Aaron, H.J. (1978). *Politics and Professors: The Great Society in Perspective.* Washington, D.C.: Brookings Institution.

Abramson, L. Y., and M. E. Seligman (1978). "Learned Helplessness in Humans: Critique and Reformation." *Journal of Abnormal Psychology* 87 (1), 49–74.

Akhtar, S. (1983). "The Concept of Splitting and Its Clinical Relevance." *American Journal of Psychiatry* 140 (8), 1013–1016.

Alcohol, Drug Abuse, and Mental Health Administration (1980), p. 549.

Allen, N. H. (1980). *Homicide Perspectives on Prevention New York*: Human Sciences Press.

Allport, G. W. (1954). *The Nature of Prejudice.* Cambridge, Massachusetts: Addison-Wesley Publishing Company, Inc.

American Psychiatric Association (1994). *Diagnostic and Statistical Manual of Mental Disorders* (ed. 4). Washington, DC: American Psychiatric Association.

Anderson, E. (1994). "The Code of the Streets." *The Atlantic Monthly* 4, 81–94.

Bach-y-Rita, G., and J. R. Lion (1971) "Episodic Dyscontrol: A Study of 130 Violent Prisoners." *American Journal of Psychiatry* 127, 1473–1478.

Balkwell, J. W. (1990). "Ethnic Inequality and the Rate of Homicide." *Social Forces* 69, 53–70.

Bandura, A. (1969). *Principles of Behavior Modification*. New York: Holt, Rinehart and Winston.

Banks, W. C. (1976). "White Preference in Blacks: A Paradigm in Search of a Phenomenon." *Psychological Bulletin* 83 (6), 1179–1186.

Bass, B. A., G. E. Watt, and G.J. Powell (1982). *The Afro-American Family*. New York: Grune and Stratton.

Bell, C. (1987). *Preventive Strategies for Dealing with Violence Among Blacks*. Community Mental Health, 23 (3), 217–235.

Bell, C.; and E. T. Jenkins (1993). "Community Violence and Children on Chicago's Southside." *Psychiatry* 56 (2), 46–54.

Bell, D. (1968). *Relevant Aspect of the Social Scene and Social Policy*. New York: Committee for the Children of New York.

Bau, J. R. and P. M. Blau (1982). "The Cost of Inequality: Metropolitan Structure and Violent Crime." *American Sociological Review* 47, 114–129.

Blau, Z. (1982). *Black Children/White Children: Competence, Socialization, and Social Structure.* New York: Free Press.

Bohannan, P. (1964). *African and Africans.* New York: American Museum of Science Books.

Boone, S. L. (1990). "Aggression in African American Boys: A Discriminate Analysis." *Genetic, Social, and General Psychology Monographs* 117 (2), 203–228.

Bowlby, J. (1979). *The Making and Breaking of Affectionate Bonds.* London: Tavistock Publications.

Brantley, A. C., and A. Dirosa (1994). "Gangs: A National Perspective." *FBI Law Enforcement Bulletin.*

Bromberg, W. (1961). *The Mold of Murder: A Psychiatric Study of Homicide.* New York: Grune and Stratton.

Blos, P. (1972). *On Adolescence.* New York: Free Press.

Blos (1972). *Adolescent Is Searching for Identity and Social Independence.*

Brenner, A. (1984). *Helping Children Cope with Stress.* Lexington, Massachusetts: Lexington Books.

Brenner, (1973). *Cross Generational Pattern of Stress Induction and Stress Accumulation.*

Brenns, H. (1973). *Mental Illness and the Economy*. Cambridge, Massachusetts: Harvard University Press.

Busch, K. G. (1990). "Adolescents Who Kill." *Journal of Clinical Psychology* 46 (4), 472–485.

Bushman, B. J., and H. M. Cooper (1990). "Effects of Alcohol on Human Aggression: An Integrative Research Review." *Psychological Bulletin* 107, 341–354.

Carlson, G. A. and D. P. Cantell (1980). "Unmasking Mask Depression in Children and Adolescents." *American Journal of Psychiatry* 137 (4), 415–449.

Carry, D. G. (1994). *Gang Crime and Law Enforcement Record Keeping*. US Department of Justice, Office of Justice Programs.

Centers for Disease Control and Prevention (1992). "Homicides Rates Is Highest Among African American Males."

Cesaire, A. (1972). *Discourse on Colonialism*. New York: Monthly Review Press.

Chandler (1982). "Provides Empirical Evidence Linking Specific Casual Attributions to Anger Arousal-Aggressive Responding."

Chicago Police Department (1990). "Murder Analysis." Detective Division, Chicago Police Department.

Clark, K. B. (1965). *Dark Ghetto*. New York: Harper and Row.

Cohen, C. I. (1985). "Social Networks, Stress, and Physical Health: A Longitudinal Study of an Inner-City Elderly Population." *Journal of Gerontology* 40, 476–486

Collins, J. (1986). "The Relationship of Problem Drinking to Individual Offending Sequences." Vol. 2, Washington, DC: National Academy Press.

Collins, K. A. (1993). "A Retrospective and Prospective Study of Cerebral Tissue Pulmonary Embolism in Severe Head Trauma." *Journal of Forensic Science* 39 (3), 624–628.

Comer, J. P., and A. F. Poussaint, (1992). *Raising Black Children*. New York Penguin Books.

Cotten, N. U., et al. (1994). Aggression and fighting behavior among African American adolescents: Individual and family factors. American Journal of Public Health 84 (4), 618–622.

Coughlin, E. K. (1995) Breaking the prejudice habit. The Chronicle of Higher Education 42 (9), 12–16.

Curry, G.D., et al. (1992). "Gang Involvement and Delinquency Among Hispanics and African American Adolescent Males." *Journal of Research in Crime and Delinquency* 29, 273–291.

Curtis, L. A. (1957). *Violence, Race, and Culture*. Lexington, Massachusetts: Health.

Denton, N. A., and D. S. Massey (1988). "Residential Segregation of Blacks, Hispanics, and Asians by Socioeconomic Status and Generation." *Social Science Quarterly* 69, 797–817.

Derezotes, D. (1995). "Evaluation of Late-Night Basketball Project." *Child and Adolescent Social Work Journal*, 12 (1), 33–50.

Deutsch (1993). "Reported African American Children Had More Negative Self-Images than Did White Children."

Dodge, K. A. (1981). "Biased Decision-Making Processes in Aggressive Boys." *Journal of Abnormal Psychology* 90, 375–379.

Dohrenwend, B. S., and B. P. Dohenwend (1970). "Class and Race as Status-Related Sources of Stress." *Social Stress*, Chicago: Alden, pp. 111–140.

DuBois, W. E. B. (1904). *The Souls of Black Folk*. New York: New American Library.

Dukes (1985). "The Healthy Single Parent and Support Network from an Extended Family Can Result in Healthy Family Functioning."

Durant, R. H., R. A. Pendergast and C. Cadenhead (1994). "Exposure to Violence and Victimization and Fighting Behavior by Urban Black Adolescents." *Journal of Adolescent Health* 15, 311–318.

Durant, R. H., et al. (1995). *Developmental and Behavioral Pediatrics*, 16 (4), 233–237.

Easson, W. M. (1977). "Depression in Adolescence." *Adolescent Psychiatry. Vol. V. Developmental and Clinical Studies*. New York: Analytic Press.

Ebata (1990). "Stress Component in Adjustment in African American Males in High Crime Areas. Lack of Mature Cognitive Coping Skills."

Black Male Youth (1999). "Boston Police Stopping African American Youth When Leaving School."

Erickson, E. H. (1963). *Childhood and Society*. New York: W.W. Norton & Co.

Eron, L. D., J. H. Gentry, and P. Schlegel (1994). *Reason to Hope: A Psychosocial Perspective on Violence and Youth*. Washington, D. C.: American Psychological Association.

Festinger, L. (1954). "A Theory of Social Comparison Processes." *Human Relations* 7, 177.

Fitzpatrick, K. M., and J. P. Boldizar (1993). "The Prevalence and Consequences of Exposure to Violence Among African American Youth." *Journal of American Academy of Child and Adolescent Psychiatry* 32 (2), 424–430.

Fondacaro, M. R., and K. Heller (1990). "Attributional Style in Aggressive Adolescent Boys." *Journal of Abnormal Child Psychology* 18 (1), 75–89.

Franklin, N. C. (1989). *Black Families in Therapy: A Multi-Systems Approach*. New York: The Guilford Press.

Franklin-Boyd, N. (1982). *Black Families in Therapy*. New York.

Frazier, E. F. (1939). *The Negro Family in the United States*. Chicago: University of Chicago Press.

Freud, S. (1953). *Standard Edition of the Complete Psychological Works of Sigmund Freud*. (Vols. 1–23). London: Hogarth Press.

Gibbs, J. T. (1984). "Black Adolescents and Youth: An Endangered Species." *American Journal of Orthopsychiatry* 54, 6–22.

Giddings, P. (1984). *When and Where I Enter*. New York: William Morrow.

Giovachinni, P. L. (1977). "Psychoanalytic Perspective on Adolescence, Psychic Development, and Narcissism." *Adolescent Psychiatry. Vol. V. Developmental and Clinical Studies*. New York: Jason Arnson, pp. 113–1410.

Gladstein,J., E.J. Rusonis, and F. P. Heald (1992). "A Comparison of Inner City and Upper Middle-Class Youth's Exposure to Violence." *Journal of Adolescent Health* 13, 275–280.

Gordon, C. (1969). *Looking Ahead*. Washington, D.C.: American sociological Association.

Greene, M. B. (1993). "Chronic Exposure to Violence and Poverty: Interventions that Work for Youth." *Crime and Delinquency* 39 (1), 106–124.

Grier, W. H., and P. M. Cobbs (1968). "Fathers Absence Has Detrimental Effect on Children." *Black Rage*. New York: Basic Books. Griggs (1968)

Griflin, J. T. (1991). "Racism and Humiliation in the African American Community." *Journal of Primary Prevention* 12 (2), 149–167.

Hacker, A. (1992). *Two Nations: Black and White, Separate, Hostile, and Unequal*. New York: MacMillan.

Hammond, W. R., and B. Yung (1993). "Psychology's Role in Public Health Response to Assaultive Violence Among Young African American Men." *American Psychologist* 48 (2), 142–154.

Harer, M. D., and D. Steffensmeier (1992). "The Differing Effects of Economic Inequality on Black and White Rates of Violence." *Social Forces* 70 (4), 1035–1054.

Harper, F. D. (1976). *Alcohol Abuse and Black America*. Alexandria, Virginia: Douglas.

Hartnagel, T. F. (1970). "Father Absence and Self-Conception Among Lower Class White and Negro Boys." *Social Problem* 18, 152–163.

Hartnagel (1970). "Self-Concept Lowered When African American Male Father Absent."

Herkovits, M. J. (1958). *Cultural Anthropology*. New York: Knopf.

Hogan, D. P. and E. Kitagawa (1985). "The Impact of Social Status, Family Structure, and Neighborhood on the Fertility of Black Adolescents." *American Journal of Sociology* 90, 825–855.

Huges, S. O. (1989). "Defining Patterns of Drinking in Adolescents: A Cluster Analytic Approach." *Journal of Studies on Alcohol* 53 (1).

Humphrey, J. A. (1987). "Stressful Life Events and Criminal Homicide." *Omega* 17 (4).

Ilfeld, F. W. (1977). "Current Social Stressors and Symptoms of Depression." *American Journal of Psychiatry* 134, 161–166.

Ilfeld, F. W. (1978). "Psychological Status of Community Residents Along Major Demographic Dimensions." *Archives of General Psychiatry* 35, 716–724.

Inciardi, J. (1992). "The Crack-Violence Connection." *Journal of Drug Issues* 16, 92–111. Institute on Black Chemical Abuse (1990). Minneapolis, Minnesota.

Jenkins, A. H. (1982). *The Psychology of the African American: A Humanistic Approach*. New York: Pergamon Press.

Jenkins, E., and C. Bell (1991). "Traumatic Stress in Children."

Journal of Health Care for the Poor and Underserved 2, 1.

Jones, R. L. (1980). *Black Psychology*. New York: Harper and Row.

Jones, R. L. (1989, 1990). *Black Adolescents*. Berkeley, California: Cobb and Henry, Publishers.

Jones, W. D. (1969). *White Over Black: American Attitudes Towards the Negro*. London: Penguin Books.

Kaplan, H. B. (1975). *Self-Attitudes and Deviant Behavior*. Pacific Palisades, California: Goodyear.

Kardiner, A., and L. Ovessey (1951). *The Mark of Oppression*. Cleveland: World.

Kasi, S., and S. Cobb (1967). "Health Behavior, Illness Behavior, and Sick Behavior." *Archives of Environmental Health* 12, 246–266.

Kaufman, J. M. (1994). "Violent Children and Youth: A Call for Attention." *Journal of Behavioral Education* 4 (2), 153–155.

Klein, M. (1986). *Assessing Object Relations Phenomena*. New York: International Universities Press.

Lane, M. P. (1989). "Inmate Gangs." *Corrections Today* 1, 98–128.

Lawson, G. W., and A. W. Lawson (1989). *Alcoholism and Substance Abuse in Special Populations*. Gaithersburg, Maryland: Aspen Publishing, Inc.

Lazarus, R. S., and S. Folkman (1982). *Coping and Adaptation*. New York: Guilford Press, pp. 282–325.

Lewis, D. O. (1979). "Some Evidence of Race Bias in the Diagnosis and Treatment of the Juvenile Offender." *The American Journal of Orthopsychiatry*. 49, 53–61.

Linehan, M. M. (1989). "Cognitive and Behavioral Therapy for Borderline Personality Disorder." *In Review of Psychiatry*. Washington, D. C.: American Psychiatric Press, pp. 84–120.

Lopez, (1983). "Under-pathologizing Bias"

Maslow, A. H. (1967). "A Theory of Metamotivation: The Biological Rooting of the Value of Life." *Journal of Humanistic Psychology* 7, 93–127.

Massey, D. S. (1990). "The Ecology of Inequality: Minorities and the Concentration of Poverty, 1970–1980." *American Journal of Sociology* 95, 1153–1188.

McCoy, S., and D. Finkelhor (1995). "Psychosocial Sequelae of Violent Victimization in a National Youth Sample." *Journal of Consulting and Clinical Psychology* 63 (5), 726–736.

McGaha, J. E., and E. L. Leoni (1995). *Adolescence* 30 (118), 474–482.

Mead, H. (1962). *Self and Society from the Standpoint of a Social Behaviorist*. Chicago: University of Chicago Press.

Milwaukee Journal Sentinel, April 28, 1998.

Monahan, J. (1981). "The Clinical Prediction of Violent Behavior." US Department of Health and Human Services.

Morton (1980). *Self-Fulfilling Prophecy*.

Morton R. K. (1967). *Social Theory and Social Structure*. Glencoe, Illinois: Free Press of Glencoe.

Moynihan, P. D. (1965). "The Negro Family." Office of Policy Planning and Research, US Department of Labor.

Meyers, H. (1982). "Stress, Ethnicity, and Social Class. A Model for Research with Black Populations." *Minority Mental Health*. New York: Praeger, pp. 118–148.

Myers (1982). *Urban Stress Model*.

Myers, J. F., and L. M. King (1980). "Youth of the Black Underclass: Urban Stress and Mental Health." *Fanon Center Journal*, 1 (1), 1–27.

Myrdal, G. (1944). *An American Dilemma*. New York: Harper.

National Institute of Mental Health (1977). "Psychiatric Services and the Changing Institutional Scene." DHEW Pub. No. (ADM) 717–413, Series B, 12–17.

Nobles, W. (1980). "African Philosophy: Foundations for Black Psychology." In R. Jones (Ed.), *Black Psychology* (ed. 2) New York: Harper & Row, pp. 23–36.

Patterson, G. R. (1986). "Performance Models for Antisocial Boys." *American Psychologist* 41. 432–4,44.

Paster, V. S. (1985). "Adapting Psychotherapy for the Depressed, Unacculturated, Acting Out Black Male Adolescent." *Psychotherapy* 22, 408–413.

Pernanen, K. (1981). *Theoretical Aspects of the Relationship Between Alcohol and Crime*. New York: Guilford Press.

Pierce, W. J., and S. M. Singleton (1994). "Improvisation as a Concept for Understanding and Treating Violent Behavior Among African American Youth." *The Journal of Contemporary Human Services*, 444–450·.

Poussaint, A. F. (1984). "Black on Black Homicide: A Psychological Political Perspective." *Victimology* 8, 161–169.

Poussaint, A. F. (1980). "Interracial Relations and Prejudice." *Contemporary Issues in Psychiatry*, 3155–3161.

Poussaint, A. F. (1974). "The Black Child's Image of the Future." *Educational Learning for Tomorrow*, 56–71.

Pynoos, R. S., and S. Eth (1985). "Witness to Violence: The Child Interview." *Journal of the American Academy of Child Psychiatry* 25, 306–319.

Reber, A. S. (1985). *Dictionary of Psychology*. London: Penguin Books, p. 687.

Rose, H. M. (1981). "Black Homicide and the Urban Environment." Unpublished Report to Center for Minority Group Mental Health Programs, National Institute of Mental Health.

Rosella, J. D., and S. A. Albrecht (1993). "Toward an Understanding of the Health Status of Black Adolescents: An Application of the Stress-Coping Framework." *Issues in Comprehensive Pediatric Nursing* 16, 193–205.

Rosenberg, M. (1971). *Black and White Self-Esteem: The Urban School Child*. Washington, DC: American Sociological Association.

Roth, L. H. (1987). *Clinical Treatment of the Violent Person*. New York: Guilford Press.

Rutter, M. (1984). *Juvenile Delinquency: Trends and Perspectives*. New York: Guilford Press.

Salts, C. J., B. W. Linbholm, and H. W. Goddard (1995). "Predictive Variables of Violent Behavior in Adolescent Males." *Youth and Society* 26 (3), 377–399.

Sampson, R. J. (1985). "Race and Criminal Violence: A Demographically Disaggregated Analysis of Urban Homicide." *Crime and Delinquency* 31, 47–82.

Schubiner, H., R. Scott, and A. Tzelepis (1993). "Exposure to Violence Among Inner-City Youth." *Journal of Adolescent Health* 14, 214–219.

Seligman, M. E. P. (1975). *Helplessness: On Depression, Development, and Death.* San Francisco: Freeman.

Selye, H. (1956). *The Stress of Life.* New York: McGraw-Hill.

Shanok, S. S. (1983). "A Comparison of Delinquent and Nondelinquent Adolescent Psychiatric In-Patients." *American Journal of Psychiatry* 140, 582–585.

Sheley, J. F. (1993). *Gun Acquisition and Possession in Selected Juvenile Samples.* National Institute of Justice, Office of Juvenile Justice and Delinquency Prevention, 2–11.

Shneidman, E. S. (1976). "A Psychological Theory of Suicide." *Psychiatric Annals* 6, 9–121.

Silverstein. B., and R. Krate (1975). *Children of the Dark Ghetto: A Developmental Psychology.* Praeger: New York.

Sommers, I., and D. R. Basking (1994). "Factors Related to Female Adolescent Initiation into Violent Street Crime." *Youth and Society* 25 (4.), 468–489.

Spencer, M. B. (1988). "Racial Attitude and Self-Concept Development in Black Children." Paper Presented at the Meeting of the American Orthopsychiatric Association, Washington, D.C., March 21–25, 1975.

Spitz, R. (1950). "The Psychopathic Delinquent Child: Possible Infantile Precursors of Psychopathology." *American Journal of Orthopsychiatry* 20, 223–265.

Spunt, B., et al. (1994). "Alcohol and Homicide: Interviews with Prison Inmates." *The Journal of Drug Issues* 24 (1), 143–163.

Spunt, B. (1990). "Race, Ethnicity, and Gender Differences in the Drugs-Violence Relationship." *Journal of Psychoactive Drugs* 22, 293–303.

Spunt (1990). *Conducted Interviews with 268 Homicide Offenders in New York State Correctional Facility*. Pick Up Book at Library.

Staples, R. (1990). "Substance and the Black Family Crisis: An Overview." *The Western Journal of Black Studies* 14 (4).

Staples, R. (1982). *Black Masculinity: The Black Male's Role in American Society*. San Francisco: Black Scholar Press.

Sullivan, H. S. (1972). *Personal Psychopathology*. New York: W.W. Norton & Company.

Sullivan, H. S. (1971). *The Fusion of Psychiatry and Social Science*. New York: W. W. Norton & Company.

Takata, S. R. (1992). *Metropolitan Gang Influence and the Emergence of Group Delinquency in a Regional Community*. Kenosha, Wisconsin: Department of Sociology, University of Wisconsin-Parkside.

Terr, L. (1989). "Consultation Advised Soon After Child's Psychic Injury." *Clinical Psychiatric Times* 17 (5).

Terrell, F. (1975). "The Development of an Inventory to Measure Certain Aspects of Black Nationalist Ideology." Paper Presented at the Eastern Psychological Association Convention.

Turner (1984). "Maladaptive Schemas US Bureau of the Census (1980)." Census of Population: Vol. 1, part 51, General Social and Economic Characteristics. Washington, DC: US Government Printing Office.

Ward, J. V. (1995). "Cultivating a Morality of Care in African American Adolescents: A Culture-Based Model of Violence Prevention." *Harvard Educational Review* 65 (2), 175–188.

Watts, G. E. (1978). "A Comparison of the Scaling of Afro-American Life Change Events." *Journal of Human Stress* 3, 13–18.

Weiner, B., S. Graham, and C. Chandler (1982). "Pity, Anger, and Guilt: An Attributional Analysis." *Personality and Social Psychology Bulletin* 8, 226–232.

Whaley, A. L. (1992). "A Culturally Sensitive Approach to Prevention of Interpersonal Violence Among Urban Black Youth. *Journal of the National Medical Association* 84 (7), 585–588.

White, H., J. Brick, and S. Hansell (1993). "A Longitudinal Investigation of Alcohol Use and AGGRESSION in adolescence." *Journal of Studies on Alcohol* 11, 62–77.

White, H. R. (1990). "Longitudinal Stability and Dimensional Structure of Problem Drinking in Adolescence." *Journal of Studies on Alcohol* 48, 541–550.

White, J. L., and T. A. Parham (1990). *The Psychology of Blacks: An African American Perspective*. Englewood Cliffs, New Jersey: Prentice Hall.

Whitehead, T. L. (1993). "The Hustle, Socioeconomic Deprivation, Urban Drug Trafficking, and Low Income African American Male Gender Identity." *Pediatrics* 93 (6), 1050–1054.

Wieczorek, W. (1990). "Alcohol, Drugs, and Murder: A Study of Convicted Homicide Offenders." *Journal of Criminal Justice* 18, 217–227.

Wilson, J. W. (1987). *The Truly Disadvantaged: The Inner City, the Underclass, and Public Policy*. Chicago: The University of Chicago Press.

Winnicott, D. W. (1968). *The Family and Individual Development*. New York: Routledge, Chapman & Hall, Inc.

Winnicott, D. W. (1967). "Delinquency as a Sign of Hope." Lecture Given to Borstal Assistant Governor's Conference, King Alfred's College, Winchester, England, 1967.

Winnicott, D. W. (1984). *Deprivation and Delinquency*. New York: Tawistock Publications.

Wisconsin Office of Justice Assistance (1985). "Crime and Arrests." Madison, Wisconsin: State of Wisconsin.

Wishner, A. R., et al. (1991). "Interpersonal Violence-Related Injuries in an African American Community in Philadelphia." *American Journal of Public Health* 81, 1474–1476.

Young, J. E. (1993). *Reinventing Your Life: How to Break Free of Negative Life Patterns*. New York: Dutton.

Young, R. A. (1984). "Using the Theory of Reasoned Action to Improve the Understanding of Recreational Behavior." *Journal of Leisure Research* 17, 90–106.

ABOUT THE AUTHOR

BORN IN FAIRHOPE, Alabama, Dr. Bracy has lived in Milwaukee, Wisconsin, for over twenty-five years. He earned his BA at the University of Wisconsin, Milwaukee, after an associate's degree from the Milwaukee Area Technical College. His master's degree and doctorate, both in clinical psychology, were earned at the Illinois School of Professional Psychology. Dr. Bracy is now in private practice in the Milwaukee area and is a consulting psychologist as well.

"Black teenagers have been killing each other at an alarming rate in major cities across the United States," Dr. Bracy says. "Because of these murders, we are losing some of our most precious natural resources (the children). In working with teenagers, I have come up with many plausible explanations."

This book is the result.